MY LIFE ON THE CROOME ESTATE

Hope you enjoy my story.

Malcolm Walford.

20/1/22.

My Life on the Croome Estate

Malcolm Walford

My Life on the Croome Estate
Malcolm Walford

Published by Aspect Design 2013
Malvern, Worcestershire, United Kingdom.

Designed, printed and bound by Aspect Design
89 Newtown Road, Malvern, Worcs.WR14 1PD
United Kingdom
Tel: 01684 561567
E-mail: allan@aspect-design.net
Website: www.aspect-design.net

Cover Design © 2013 Aspect Design
Original photographs © Malcolm Walford © 2013
ISBN 978-1-908832-50-4

Foreword

I have written this book in memory of Maria, Lady Coventry. At a lunch held in the RAF Canteen at Croome in 2007, Lady Maria was informed by Mr Peter Beresford that the Croome Estate Trustees had bought Croome Court and had set up the Croome Heritage Trust. Lady Maria, who was born at Croome Court was overjoyed with this wonderful news.

Unfortunately Lady Maria never got the chance to visit her old home as she passed away later in 2007.

A wonderful lady who is so very sadly missed.

M.W.

Acknowledgments

I would like to thank the Croome Estate Trustees who first asked me to gather these memoirs together, Alice Padley of the National Trust who has helped me considerably over the last twelve months and finally my partner Gaynor Powell for all the hard work she has carried out in putting my memoirs into some sort of order.

My name is Malcolm Walford and I was born, and spent my early years, in Wednesfield, Wolverhampton. Due to family commitments my father decided, in early 1948, that my parents, my brother and myself, should move to Wadborough, near Worcester, to live with, and look after, his mother. I was fifteen years old when we moved into Rose Cottage, Pirton Sidings, Wadborough to live with my gran. The house was then owned by the Croome Estate as my late grandfather had been a drainer on the Estate.

The cottage is now privately owned and known by its former name, Perry Wood End.

Life at Wadborough was very peaceful, not many cars about, only the local delivery vans. During the war years when we had come on holiday to gran's, you could wake up in the morning, look out of the bedroom window, and see the soldiers from Norton Barracks pass by on their route march. You could also watch the aircraft taking off and landing at RAF Defford. During these visits, dad would sometimes go off plum picking to earn an extra bit of cash. He was very good at this because he was born a country lad. He had six sisters and two brothers, how the family managed I do not know. We spent some wonderful times with my gran, and although, at the time, I was always glad to get home to the Station House at Wednesfield, I am now even gladder that dad and mum made that momentous decision to move to Wadborough to look after gran.

The cottage was situated not far from the LMS main line from Birmingham to Bristol. The sidings consisted of a cattle dock, signal box and a small cottage. The crossing gates were operated from the signal box where the signalman, or 'Bobbie', would turn a very large wheel to open and close the gates. There were three signalmen working in shifts; from 6am to 2pm, two to ten and then ten to six. Their names, I recall, were Jackie Brown, who lived in Wadborough, Bert Corbett, who lived at Drakes Broughton and Cliff Jones who lived in the small cottage by the sidings gate. There were also a porter and a lorry driver stationed at the sidings, the lorry driver's name was Walter Reynolds and before we moved in with gran, he used to lodge with her.

When we were young we used to venture into Perry Wood, a large area of woodland in front of the cottage which stretched from Panfield, on the Croome Pershore Road, across to Pirton. This was the Wadborough side of Pirton and the LMS railway line ran straight through this large wooded area. There was a house by the side of the railway line in the middle of the wood called Clarke's Crossing. Mrs Clarke and several of her daughters lived in the tiny cottage. The cottage was there to let the Croome Hounds cross the line when the hunt was about. I am sorry to say that old Mrs Clarke, the crossing keeper, was knocked down and killed by an express train back in the 1950s. There were gates both sides of the railway line and with steam engines still in use on the railway at this time, there were often lineside fires. When these occurred the men from the Croome Estate forestry department would be called out with proper tools called 'Beaters' to attack the fire until the local fire brigade arrived. My father Len could recall when Perry Wood was a standing wood before it was all felled and replanted. The main drive from Pirton to Panfield was repaired using burnt soil and my Dad said workmen were there for weeks. He would not have been very old at that time so it must have been sometime in the early 1900s. There used to be a stream running through the wood where you could collect lovely watercress. We would also go onto the railway embankment and pick wild strawberries and collect nuts off the trees when the season came around.

In front of the cottage there was a field which was called 'The Common'. It was here that we held our football games. During the summer the field was put down to mowing grass so we had to keep out, but as soon as the farmer, Mr Bert Kitchener, had cut the grass we were immediately back in there. Other times we would play in an orchard in Wadborough village, which was called 'Workman's Orchard' and had some old buildings nearby which we went into if it rained. At the age of fifteen, in 1948, I and some of my mates ventured into the pub, The Masons Arms, a lovely old pub in which, over the years, I have spent many a happy hour. I know we should not have been in the pub at that age but if the local 'bobby' came we used to slip out the back of the pub and into Narrow Wood – happy days.

I first went to Pirton Pool when I was aged fifteen. We kids, from Wadborough Youth Club, used to bike there on a Sunday afternoon, some of the lads swam in the pool near the old culvert. I think they called it sandy bay but I don't know why. Others of us played football and messed about with the girls. They were great summer afternoons.

We lads of Wadborough would all meet up at the Mason's Arms and have a few jugs, before making our way across Workman's Orchard to Wadborough Hut where, at that time, the dances were held. There was no band, just Ron Thompson and his old time records. Here we would meet up with our young lady friends. The girls would come on their bikes, no cars in those days, and would travel from all around, Pershore, Defford, Drakes Broughton, Stoulton, Littleworth and Norton, and a good night would be had by all. Sometimes we would escort the girls home but we never got close to their houses because their fathers would be waiting up for them, so we kept clear. I went out with a girl from Abbotswood for some time. We were getting pretty strong until one night I was invited indoors and her Mom started talking about us getting engaged. I wasn't ready to settle down yet so things came to a stop.

My late gran would not have a bad word said against either the workmen or any member of staff of the Estate. Mind you, living in a tied cottage belonging to the Estate, you had to be wary of what you said. My granddad died before I knew him. My family goes back a long way, serving the Croome Estate.

Wadborough, like most villages, has changed and a lot of my mates have sadly passed on, I think there are only two of them still living in the village. I sometimes forget we are all getting older. I am just lucky, at nearly eighty, to be active and still involved with old Estate properties and Croome Court.

One of the tales my Dad, Len Walford, told happened in the 1940s, during the time when he was in the forestry department. He, my uncle Bob and Jim Hemming, were at work in the Ridings, near the southern end of Defford Airfield, busy thinning out. Uncle Bob had an old Austin Seven but Dad and Jim always biked to work. One lunchtime, they bundled into Bob's motor and went to the Cider House at Woodmancote (it was known as the Monkey House). Bob and Jim had too much cider and once back in the wood, lay down and went to sleep! It was a good job my dad was awake because Col. Osbert Smith decided to visit them. Jim and Bob took some waking, but, much to his relief, dad got them alert enough to grab hold of their clearing tools and start work. The next day they stayed well clear of the Cider House!

RAF Defford 1948-53

When I worked at RAF Defford, before I started with the Estate, I was employed by the station contractors, Lewis & Watters Ltd, a very large company from Leamington Spa. I should think there were fifty men employed at the Camp. The firm was also station contractor at RAF Tilesford not far from Pershore. My boss was a man named Arthur Palmer. My job then was dealing with the stores and assisting Arthur Palmer with any measuring on sites. Although the firm had vehicles Arthur and I always used our push bikes to get to the various sites, whether it be down at the south end of the camp or up to Croome or into Perry Wood. Some days we would be at the Officers Mess at Croome which was situated in the grounds of Croome Court. Also in the grounds were a dance hall, picture house, NAAFI and a fish and chip shop.

To the south west of Defford Airfield were two large hangars together with various other buildings. This part of the Camp was the Servicing Wing for all aircraft, a very busy part of the complex. At the centre was the joiners' workshop where all the patterns were made before the actual radar cones were manufactured and fitted to the planes. To the south east there was another large aircraft hangar. Lewis and Watters had the task of excavating the floors inside the hangar. This was so that a weighbridge could be put in to weigh the various aircraft. As the old deer park was very wet and boggy, we had to hire several pumps to keep the water level down. The pumps and the workmen worked all through the night to complete the works. Once this was accomplished concreting proceeded. The concrete was mixed using large concrete mixers (no Readymix at this time). Then the brickwork was started, the walls rendered and 'Pudlo' waterproofer was applied. In time the works were completed and eventually the weighbridge was fitted.

During a visit I made some months later there was a Wellington Bomber sitting on the weighbridge and I was asked by the RAF mechanic if I would like to have a look inside. Scrambling through the aircraft my thoughts were of the young RAF bomber crews who not only flew these aircraft during the war but also, in some cases, lost their lives. It does not bear to think too much of what they would have gone through if their aircraft was hit. They were very brave lads and we should always be proud of them. My cousin was a rear gunner in a Wellington during the second World War and, I'm sorry to say, never returned to his parents and sister.

The very first jet plane I saw at Defford was a Vampire. When it had landed it taxied onto an apron not far from our builders' workshop. When the pilot swung the plane round, the force of the engine lifted the tarmac off the apron and blew it against the radar section building. It was a good job there was perspex in the windows and not glass. It made yet another job for the builders, all the aprons had to have the tarmac chipped off down to the concrete base. A lot of the men got very burnt faces through chipping this tarmac off with just picks, and I remember Arthur Palmer having to go to a chemist to buy some cream for them. We carried out lots of works to the radar buildings which all had scanners in the windows. We also worked on the police huts down the Croome Road, and at the new hospital in the centre of the camp and on the control tower. It was all very interesting. I have peddled my way all around Defford Camp! One Bank Holiday we were asked to repaint the lines down the main runway using four inch paintbrushes, then to work at getting the camp spick and span for the Queen's visit. I got lumbered with painting the main gates, still it was all in a day's work. I don't think Her majesty noticed the gates as she went past very quickly.

I was also at Defford when two new hangars were built by other contractors before the firm I worked for had to complete the work. A railway line was installed in one hangar and a large winch was fitted outside. The aircraft were then winched up the concrete apron, put on skids, and pulled sideways into the hangar. The hangars were removed when Defford closed down. There were tons of concrete laid. It was all mixed using large hopper mixers worked by navvies, the sort of men you didn't want to get on the wrong side of! The builders' workshops and compound were situated not far from the control tower and perimeter track where the aircraft would taxi from their dispersal pads before making their way to the end of the runways from where they would take off.

In the early 1960s a new grain store was built on the site of the two removed hangars to serve Croome Farm. The Croome Estate Building Department erected the concrete block walls and other building works.

The War Department Police were housed in huts some way down the Croome Road. The stone wall to the park has now been reinstated. All the huts had small 'tortoise' stoves and burned coke or coal from the big fuel store at Croome near Stone Cottage where Reg Child lived with his parents. The concrete road at the side of the cottage and bases which were put in when the camp was built are still there, but the security fences and gates have long gone. Many of the rooms at the Hospital Site, the wards etc, were also fitted with these 'tortoise' stoves. Situated at the top of the main drive to Croome Court, on the right hand side, was the Officer's Mess together with various other buildings and a swimming pool.

I think I have been to all the buildings at Croome at some time or another, including the Hospital Building. I never thought then that I would, in the future, be spending a lot of my time at Croome Estate in charge of the Main Stores.

There was a department on the camp whose men used to go around the camp in their lorry collecting the toilet buckets. They were then taken to an area near the Salvation Army canteen building, opposite the main gate of Defford camp, and emptied into a sluice, and the buckets washed out ready for another day.

I have seen quite a few crashes at Defford. The first one I saw happened when I was getting ready to go home in the evening, and involved a Meteor jet plane coming in to land from the north. The main Birmingham to Bristol railway line ran just beyond the main runway and just as the local stopping train was going by, the Meteor approached too low and its nose wheel hit the top of the cab of the railway engine, breaking one of the jet's wheels off. It flew around the airfield a couple of times and then landed on the grass area with its other two wheels up, in other words the pilot made a belly landing. Amazingly, no-one was hurt, but the driver and fireman of the locomotive had to be taken off at Defford station suffering from shock. A very lucky escape for all. The second plane crash I saw was that of an English Electric Canberra which could not get its landing nose wheel down. After flying around the airfield for some considerable time in order to use up fuel and allow the Station's fire engines to get in position, the plane came to land on two wheels on the main runway, which was one and three quarter miles long. The pilot held the nose up then slowly lowered it down onto the runway with a shower of sparks flying about but the fire engines were there as soon as it stopped. Again, no one was hurt. Our builders were working on the end of this runway putting down some new concrete bays. They and the plant they were using were moved very quickly. The third plane I saw crash was a naval aircraft, a Spearfish. This plane was on test and had been doing circuits and bumps most of the day. Then the final time it came in, the undercarriage just gave way and the plane broke up. Thankfully, again, no one was hurt.

The fourth incident involved a two seater Mosquito which had an engine fire. It landed on the grass and both crew jumped out and ran. The fire brigade was again very quickly on the scene. There was never a dull moment at Defford.

Also on site were a blacksmiths shop, a cycle shop where people could borrow a push bike to get around the camp, a large cable shop where lots of women were employed making up all sorts of cabling for the aircraft, time and pay offices, administration offices, M.T. buildings and a fire engine station. There were also, of course, fire engines stationed at the control tower.

When the Queen Mother visited Cheltenham Races, her plane, a highly polished Vickers Viking, would land at Defford and was then stored at the west end of the airfield. It would be serviced, cleaned and refuelled and sentries posted over it. Many members of the Royal Family landed at Defford over the years.

On the Croome Road there was a large canteen, tennis courts and another hospital. The main guardroom was situated just inside the main gates to the Camp with a sentry box next to the iron gates. At the centre of the Camp was the Parachute Section, Royal Navy Section and a building housing the Link Trainers, and another housing the telephone exchange.

Perry Wood is not far from Panfield railway bridge. There were several RAF buildings in this wood where the Dog Section was stationed. Near the house at the entrance to Perry Wood was an anti-aircraft gun post. This would be covering Defford RAF Camp and airfield. On the Croome side of the railway bridge was a large WAAF site which has now been cleared and has reverted to agricultural land. Around the camp were a lot of notices stating that all the timber, meaning the trees, was the property of the Croome Estate. There was a road linking the top of Croome Park to the RAF Camp, where there was always a sentry on duty. This road was nicknamed the Burma Road. As you can see, there were lots of buildings in Croome Park.

The slaughterhouse was opposite Stone Cottage at Croome and very close to the sharp bend in the road. This road was altered during RAF days and the bend was cut back and a wooden pegged fence put up. The slaughterhouse building was taken down not long after I started work on the Estate and all the slates and bricks were salvaged. I think the orchard was ripped up in the 1960s to make way for growing wheat and other crops. Opposite Corner Cottage, Croome d'Abitot was another RAF site. The wrought iron fencing which sat on the boundary wall to Croome Court was, I think, taken down during the second World War, but the gates were not. These gates were eventually discovered in the long grass during the 1970s.

Severn Site was opposite Fred Gerrard's home, the Corner Cottage at Croome. If you came from High Green the buildings were right in front of you when you got to the T-junction. I think this site is where all the washing facilities were for the RAF staff.

Near the entrance road to the Hospital Site buildings was a fire picket post which was staffed by RAF Personnel. There was also a large underground water tank which must have been filled in when the picket post was demolished.

At Besford, not far from the water tower, were several wooden radar masts which were also staffed by RAF personnel. On top of Bredon Hill there were large red lights warning aircraft of the danger of high ground and also warning lights along the ridge leading from Croome Court to the Owls House to warn aircraft landing on Defford runway. I am glad I have been able to remember quite a lot of my days at Defford RAF camp and more about my working life at Croome Estate.

I list below the names of some of the men I worked with when I started my employment for Lewis & Watters, Station Contractors at RAF Defford in 1948:

LEWIS & WATTERS	AIR MINISTRY	AIRFIELD MAINTENANCE
Major Dominic	Mr Drew	Jim Sherwood
Bill Satchwell	Mr Kitchen	Denty Cotterill
George Satchwell	Peter Goodhall	
Arthur Palmer	Ken Radburn	
Harry Phipps	Arthur Griffiths	
John Pumphrey	Danny Shepard	
Bill Camb	Frank Ballard	
Bill Watts	Charlie Ambler	
Jim Robins	Arthur Goodhall	
Arthur Sheward Snr	Charlie Panting	
Arthur Sheward Jnr	Charlie Beresford	
Charlie Bayliss	George Goodhall	
Albert Quarrel	Harry Skillern	
Ernest Haynes	Jack Taylor	
George Crompton		
Arthur Neathway		

At this time, at Croome, on the High Green side of the old iron bridge before you would get to the bridge side walls on the right, were a pair of wrought iron gates leading up to Croome Church. They were still in place when I started work on the Estate. These gates were similar to a pair which led from the Church Cover into the grounds of Croome Court. I was always told that the gates leading to the Church had been called the funeral gates but when Lady Maria Coventry got married, she went this way and because the ground was so wet, a tractor had to be called to pull her vehicle across the grounds.

The gates to each side of the piers of the Punch Bowl gates at Boat House cover were removed during the Second World War to assist with the war effort, but I can just remember one of these gates which was off a pattern of the old gates stored in the blacksmith's shop at High Green yard. I think this also went for scrap during the Estate yard stores improvements during 1968/69. The wrought iron fencing which sat on the boundary wall to Croome Court, near the London or Marble Arch, was also removed during the Second World War but the gates remained and were later found in the long grass during the 1970s.

The Game Keeper's Cottage was situated near the footpath leading to Croome Church. Before my time at Croome there used to be a weighbridge on the side of the road, used by local farmers to weigh fruit before it was taken to Pershore Market or the Railway Yard at Pirton Sidings. I think the building which was used to house the machinery is still standing. When the weighing machine collapsed some years ago the hole was filled in and is now grassed over.

Originally there were two pairs of statues, one either side of the front of the Temple Greenhouse in Croome Park, one each side of the dwarf walls. I was told by Fred Gerrard that during the second World War, thieves came one night to remove the lead lined statues to sell for their scrap value. The heads and arms were cut off the statues which were then rolled across the grass in front of the Temple Greenhouse and dropped over the ha-ha wall. However the thieves could not get them up the embankment. By luck one of the Special Constables who were based in High Green was informed by estate employees that they had seen a lorry travelling along Westfield Lane. He informed the other constables; Mr Eastment, Mr Faithfull, Mr Charlie Jones and Jess Gerrard, and the thieves were caught red handed. The damaged statues were then retrieved and stored in a garage belonging to the Head Forester at No. 6 High Green including all parts that had been cut off. They were stored in this garage for some years until in the eighties the third Lady Coventry saw them and asked if they could be repaired, because she would like them at Earls Croome Court where a new feature garden and fish pools had been built. I had to find all the odd pieces of scrap lead I could and then we moved the statues, with the help of the front end loader on our tractor, into the joiners' workshop. In order to make them safe we roped them to the beams in the workshop. Reg Child, whose father had been the Estate blacksmith for many years, was responsible for carrying out the repairs and made a wonderful job of getting all the dents out and refixing the heads and arms. Lady Coventry was very pleased with the results and sent a letter to Reg saying what a great job he had done. Once the statues were completed, the time came to move them to their position at Earls Croome Court. We had to hire a JCB from Zenith Plant in Pershore in order to load the statues onto our tractor trailer together with scaffold planks and boarding to lay on the lawns so as not to leave tyre marks when we unloaded the statues. All went well and the statues were placed in their new positions. Unfortunately, some years later, both statues were stolen, never to be seen again, so after all our hard graft someone else has the benefit of all Reg Child's great work.

High Green was a sleepy little village, but there was a lot of activity when Defford Airfield was being built and the RAF Vehicles started appearing. There were lots of coaches bringing civilian workers to the airfield. Then when the M5 motorway was under construction, all the heavy lorries would come through the village to go to the old RAF Buildings at Croome which were being used as their repair garages. Monks, the contractors, used to call at the little shop at High Green and collect supplies, tea, coffee etc. Some days there would be as many as six or seven lorries parked outside the shop which was based at No. 8 High Green.

The Coventry Arms, High Green Village

This was also an off licence. When I started at Croome in 1953 the owner/tenant was a Mr Hyman. Living with him, at that time, were his daughter and son-in-law, their name was Muggleston and they came originally from Leicestershire. Mr Muggleston kept a few beef cows and also some milking cattle. There was quite a bit of land belonging to the pub so it was run like a smallholding. The vegetable garden was kept in tip-top condition, not a weed to be seen anywhere. They grew all their own vegetables.

The local menfolk would meet in the pub at night and there were seats and tables outside where you could drink your beer if it was dry; but if it became wet, Mr Hyman used to let them come into his big old kitchen. But they had to be careful that the local bobby, Mr Benbow did not catch them. He was pretty keen about keeping things in proper order, but I never heard of anyone getting fined. The pub had been used as the headquarters and changing rooms when Croome United 1919, for whom my father played in goal, used to play in a field down Westfield Lane. The pub was closed down in the 1960s and the building split into two properties and at one time, a Mr Reece, a forester at the Estate lived there.

The Coventry Arms signboard which used to hang on the front of the building was, I am sure, put in the loft above the Estate Agent's Office/Muniment Room, but I cannot say if it is still there.

When my brother and I lived at Rose Cottage, in 1950, we used to go, always on a Sunday night, to the Picture House at Croome belonging to the RAF, we used to bike there. We waited by the gate at Rose Cottage until all the other lads and girls came from

Wadborough village. With their dynamo lights on their bikes, and ringing their bells – what a wonderful sight. Those boys and girls were all part of Wadborough Youth Club.

The Queen's Coronation

My late father, Len, was put in charge of all the activities regarding the celebrations which took place at Croome Court. He arranged all the sports and booked the artists for the evening Concert, which was held in the old RAF picture house building.

My parents were wonderful people, both were very hard working. They looked after my brother who suffered from quite severe eczema all his life, although he never complained. I miss them all.

Although I have had a wonderful life, one of my main regrets is that I was not deemed fit, in 1950, for National Service in the RAF due to my asthma.

Croome Estate

On 24 August 1953 I started work on the Croome Estate after the firm I was working for at RAF Defford closed down. RAF Defford was closed because the runways there were not long enough to take the new V bombers. I was single when I joined Croome and still living with my parents and brother at Rose Cottage, Pirton Sidings, Wadborough. I was courting my future wife, Mary Perks, whom I had met when we were both working at RAF Defford. Mary lived with her parents and sisters at Tanhouse Lane, Malvern Link.

Malcolm Walford with Ben, outside The Masons Arms, Wadborough, 1953

When I reported to the Estate Yard that day, I had the impression that I had gone back in time. I got the job on the Estate through my Uncle Bob who was a Forester there. After an interview with the then Agent Col. Osbert Smith, I was offered the job. On that first day, I went down to the Estate Yard on my BSA 250 motorbike and parked it by the carpenter's shop. I arrived at 7.30 am prompt wearing a brand new pair of brown bib'n'brace overalls and soon, men started to arrive for work, all on their push bikes. The first man I met that day was Fred Gerrard, who was a stonemason/bricklayer, then along came his brother, Albert, a joiner – and a very good one. Herbert Page, Tom Sherwood, Ernest Sherwood, Frank Baldwin, Charlie Jones, Reg Child, Billy Brown, George Gerrard, Brian Finch, Arthur Turk and Brian Denslow followed. There were also two blacksmiths, Tom Child and Tom Banks. And last, but not least, was Dai Partridge who was then foreman. After about an hour of my getting to know everyone, the men were ready to set off for their jobs. Two men went off pushing a sack cart with ladders on, up through High Green village. I was eventually put with Herbert Page and his labourer Tom Sherwood. High Green was a sleepy little village, all the houses were occupied by Estate employees being tied cottages which came with their jobs. I never thought at this time that in 1967 I too would be moving with my family from Pirton School into No. 8 High Green – my family's home until 1996. I will always think of No. 8 as our home. Nor did I think that I would spend so much time and become so involved with my job working for the Croome Estate Trustees.

Mr Partridge said he was going to put me with Herbert Page and Tom Sherwood the day I started and they were working at Mr Chipps' place, Sermon's Farm, Pirton which was not far from where I used to live at Rose Cottage, so I thought, I would have time to get home for dinner and come back.

I was on my motorbike and the other two were on their push bikes. They used to have to carry their tools on the handlebars. Tom Sherwood used to strap a shovel and a pick to his crossbar, and Herbert Page used to put all his bricklaying tools on his handlebars and away they went. They started off and by the time everything was sorted out I set off thirty minutes later on my motorbike and I was soon up at Ron Chipps' but they didn't arrive for another hour, I had been stood about there all that time, and I thought "What a way to carry on!". The job was to concrete a yard and I had to go and fetch a shovel from home because there were no tools, and when they had eventually got there and sorted themselves out, Tom Sherwood said they had got no petrol for the concrete mixer. I said "What do we need to do?" and they said, "one of us has to go back" and as I had got a motor bike, "could I take the two gallon can and carry it between my legs, go down to the Estate Office to get some petrol for the mixer." It was a water cooled concrete mixer then, not the new type like you have now. So I said I would go back, went to the Estate Yard, and of course by the time I got there Dai Partridge had gone out in his Ford van. I had to go into the main office and see Mr Hartland. There was a petrol pump kept on the yard for various things and it was like asking for a gallon of gold. Mr Hartland was very strict, and the men looked up to the Clerk and the bosses in those days. I said we needed petrol and had to sign the book for two gallons of petrol and then get it back to Sermons Farm. By this time it was nearly eleven o'clock and Tom Sherwood and Herbert Page had had their breakfast and of course I hadn't had mine by the time I had messed about. Anyway, we eventually started work and Tom Sherwood, said I was to mix and he would wheel, so I started mixing. I was told to slow down, I was going too fast, so I asked Tom why, and he said there was plenty of time on this job. We had dinner from one to two I think and Herbert and Tom went down under the barn on the farm and put their coats round them. I went home for dinner at one o'clock and said to dad, "Look, I can't stick this here because I've never been used to working like these men work, and it will just drive me up the wall." Anyway, by the time I'd come back from dinner, Dad had convinced me to give it a go. So, I went back to Sermons Farm and we were there for another two or three days.

I think I must have started work, not on a Monday but in the middle of week, because on the following Monday, when I went to the Estate Yard, I was told I was going to be put with a bricklayer/ stonemason whose name was Fred Gerrard who lived at Corner Cottage, Croome. Fred and I were to carry out various works on the Estate properties.

Another time I was put with the so called 'rough carpenter', a Mr Arthur Turk. The job we were sent to was at the Keeper's Cottage, (the one which used to have a weighbridge just outside the yard gates). The job was to renew both hanging posts to the yard entrance gates. First we had to excavate around the nine by nine posts to get them out, this took quite a time with just ordinary spades, grafts and bars. The posts had large butts on the ends and they took some moving (no machinery about then). After two or three days of hard slog we eventually got both posts out. Two new posts were sent up to us from the Estate yard but the new posts were longer than the ones we had removed, so we had to dig the holes deeper. Once this was done, the posts were put into position and the holes filled with clay and the clay rammed with wooden post rammers. Arthur made sure that the posts were upright ready to receive the new doors which were being made at the Estate joiners' workshop by Albert Gerrard. The old ironwork was removed from the posts and yard doors ready to re-use. I think that Albert Gerrard came and helped us fit and hang the new yard doors.

For part of this year I was working on my own. Fred Gerrard had another labourer with him. Therefore I assisted other gangs and the Estate lorry driver with any odd jobs. One of the jobs I did on my own was down at the old blacksmith forge building at Sandford, near Severn Stoke. This building was situated on the A38 adjacent to where the layby is now, at the time it was part of the main A38 road. Mr Sheppard had purchased a hand concrete block machine for the Estate which could make various sized building blocks. The machine was moved to Sandford forge complete with an old steel wheeled petrol concrete mixer which was water cooled. The old forge had two rooms which had not been used for some years. The one room housed the block machine, the other the concrete mixer. There was water laid on which you had to work by using a rotary pump. Opposite the forge were a row of black and white cottages, which were pulled down by the Estate in the 60s. My job was to make as many concrete blocks as I could in a working day. This included mixing the correct cement mix, stacking the blocks and leaving them to dry. It was an awful job working on your own. I was engaged on this job for about a month until a new bricklayer, named Sid Clifford, started on the Estate early in 1955. The machines were eventually taken to the hospital site stores at Croome and were sold at a later date.

Fred Gerrard and I did a lot of jobs together and eventually we went to Severn Bank House. Severn Bank House was used as flats during the war and the Estate was just taking it back under their control, and there was a lot of work to be done on the stonework. We didn't do this work on the stonework ourselves, Ben Davis from Worcester, the big stonemasons did that, but we did a lot of plastering and roofing, altered the kitchens and almost everything else. We did the front drive, and had to relay pebble paths and drainage works to the grounds in front of the house. One of the jobs Fred and I had to carry out was to rebuild the lovely stone wall around the property. The joints in the stonework were very thin and did not take a lot of mortar. I had to collect all the broken pieces of stone and smash them up into small pieces with a lump hammer then get an old bottle and use it like a rolling pin to crush the stone to dust. This was then mixed into the mortar so that you got a nice cream colour in the pointing.

During this time myxomatosis was rife and there were rabbits only just alive or dying all over the place, not a very nice sight to see. Fred used to kill them to put them out of their misery, but that was something I just couldn't do.

Severn Bank House took a lot of time to finish and we had two gardeners up there – Harry Corbett from Pirton, who used to be at Pirton Court as a gardener, and Jock Adams who had been the chauffeur there. They were tidying up all the gardens. The rest of the gang from the Croome Estate Building Department gradually came to Severn Bank House because there was so much work to do. There was one apprentice at the time, Brian Finch. The labourer, like myself or the apprentices who were there during dinner time, used to go right down into the bowels of the house, into the cellars, and the old staff quarters and one of us had to light a fire. We used to have an hour for dinner then and once you had had your dinner you could go for a walk or go out on to the top of the house, right on to the top of the battlements which overlooked the river Severn. The house was overlooking Malvern and the river Severn was in the field across from the house. We used to wave to the boats going down the river and then go back to work.

On the Estate we had a forty-five rung pole ladder, very heavy to raise but a wonderful ladder to work off. When working there we used to have to mix the plaster in a galvanised bucket at the rear of the house and then carry it up this ladder, which was tied to the outside of the building, to where the plasterers were working to save going through the house. Many a time I had mixed and gone up the ladder only to find the plasterer had gone off when I reached the third floor! I have also seen painters painting the outside windows (west side), with no scaffolding just planks nailed to the floor of the internal rooms. Scary, but work was always carried out successfuly.

Fred told me that when the Coventrys were at Croome Court men from the building department would have to clear any snow which was hanging off the stone parapets. I can now understand why there were so many long ladders stored at the yard, including the large, forty-five rung, pole ladder.

When Fred Gerrard and I went to Severn Bank House to join the other men who were busy doing the property up after it had been used for flats I would think it would probably be 1953/54. We heard that Mr Chesterman was going to move into the property but overnight he was relieved of his duties and was to leave Pirton Court. The next Agent to arrive was a Mr Bellingham who did move into Severn Bank House but some years later, I'm sorry to say, he was killed when serving with the territorial army.

During my time on the Estate I did many other jobs with Fred. We went to Pirton Pool before it was altered in the seventies, we had done a lot of concreting up onto the causeways. All the concrete had to be mixed by hand there because we hadn't got anything to pull the mixer up the bank with, so the gravel was taken up and we would get water out of the pool to do the concreting and, of course, we did a lot of work around the Estate before we went to Severn Bank. There was a large brick chamber not far from the causeway entrance which is now covered with large concrete slabs bedded in with cement. Inside this chamber there were several water valves. The pipework from the chamber goes down the grass slope, crosses the overflow ditch and then across to Pirton Court. There used to be some large greenhouses at Pirton Court, and this provided their water supply. These were pulled down when the Hoare family left and on the site now are two cottages. There is also a large culvert at the entrance drive to the pool. This takes a lot of stormwater from Pirton Church area. Whether it still runs, I do not know.

When working at the Lodge at Severn Stoke with Sid Clifford, Arthur Seary and Tom Sherwood, some Indian travellers came round the village trying to sell their wares. They called on us at the lodge and Arthur Seary asked one of the Indians what he had got in his suitcase. Arthur had started the ball rolling and the Indian thought he was going to make a sale. But Arthur was winding him up! When the Indian had got everything out of his suitcase, Arthur said he had decided he did not want to buy anything. The air was quite blue with the language the Indian used, but that was how Arthur Seary was – real Irish. He was eventually sacked when working at Pirton Court, demolishing some buildings. There was a row with the then Clerk of Works Mr Ken Sheppard. Mr Sheppard was threatened with a knife by Arthur, this being due to Arthur's having too much to drink, and Arthur was sacked on the spot and given notice to quit his tied cottage at Pirton.

Tommy Child was a grumpy old man but a very good blacksmith. I remember one day Reg, his son, and I had been out on a job at Severn Bank Stables fixing some new cast iron guttering. We got soaking wet due to some heavy rain, so in the afternoon, we made our way back to the yard on our bikes. Reg's dad was busy in the blacksmith's shop and told us to put our wet coats and caps by the forge and he would get them dry for us. What he did was burn our caps and singe our coats. He thought it was great fun. We didn't trust Tommy with any of our clothes after that. Tommy was a Coventry man through and through like all the old workmen. They were brought up on the Estate, and the Estate was their life.

Flower Garden Cottage at Croome d'Abitot was lived in by one of the Estate forestry workers, Jim Hemming, whose nickname, when I first started on the Estate, was 'Cracker'. He lived there with his wife and their son also named Jim. When Mr and Mrs Hemming passed on his son and wife took over the cottage. In time they moved to a new council bungalow over at Pirton, nearer to where Jim worked at Pirton Court for the farmer, Mr Jenkins. The next person to move into the cottage was a gamekeeper on the Estate.

Flooding at Severn Stoke 1953-54

The flood planks were kept in the old Saw Mills. At that time, around the Rose and Crown Public House, there were a lot of black and white cottages. It was the Estate's responsibility, in the event of flooding, to remove the families from these cottages, therefore the Estate staff were always called upon to carry out these evacuations.

I remember being called out and collecting my waders from the Estate Stores. Then we had to load the Estate wagon with various items of scaffolding to make a walkway to the cottages. After several hours, the scaffolding was erected and the people taken from their cottages. As a newcomer to the Estate, this was all very new to me, but it was a job which had to be done. What I found very difficult was the weight of the old elm boarding which was used as planking – once wet it was a ton weight, but the local people were glad to see us.

In those days there was not much wasted time, always plenty of work to be carried out on Estate properties. I did not know what to expect, but like anything else in a new job you soon find out.

Nearly all the workmen in the building department wore brown 'bib and brace' overalls with a sleeve to the trouser leg to put a Rabone ruler in, and they also all wore flat caps. When you went to work on the Estate properties, you were never allowed to wear your cap inside the property, and most of the workmen would touch the peak of their cap to the lady of the house. I was certainly learning the way things were done.

At Earls Croome Court, Lord Coventry's mother's home, you were never allowed on the property before 10 am, and never allowed to whistle or make a noise. This was Estate life and had gone on like this for a long time. Fred Gerrard, whom I worked with, told me that years ago when he was a young lad he was working with Herbert Page a bricklayer, on the front steps of Croome Court when the ninth Earl of Coventry lived there. Herbert told him that if Lady Coventry came out he was not to look at her but keep on with the job, and even when she had gone by, not to look at her.

In 1955 Mr Ken Sheppard, the then Clerk of Works, put me with a new bricklayer who had joined the staff. His name was Sid Clifford and we hit it off straight away. Some years later he left the Estate and I was then put with various other tradesmen.

During my early days at Croome I remember a brand new Parker Mini giant concrete mixer being at the Estate Yard and Mr Sheppard, the then Clerk of Works, informing me that this machine was mine and it would go where I went, to various sites. The first job Sid Clifford and I carried out was at the Estate Office, concreting the area between the Forester's Office and the then Clerk of Works Office. This mixer stayed with me through quite a lot of jobs even when I was moved to assist Fred Gerrard, it was a wonderful machine.

On the Estate at this time, the drinking wells on Estate properties were cleaned out by Estate staff. The first time I had to deal with one was when I was working with Fred Gerrard. It was at Church Farm, Pirton, the farmer's name was Mr Clift. The well was situated in the farm yard, not by the house. The Estate had a small water pump. The first job was to get a wooden pole ladder and lower it into the well, then get a piece of oak timber and put it through the top rungs, so you were safe when you climbed down the well. Next was to start the water pump and pump the water out of the well. Sometimes, if the suction pipe was not long enough, we used to have to make a timber frame over the well top and hang the pump on. Once the water was pumped out we took it in turns to go down the well with a bucket and a small shovel. The mud was then put in the bucket and hoisted to the top, then returned down the well. There was never a rope tied to the man down the well. Once all the mud was cleared the well was filled with chloride of lime, which was left for a couple of days until the well filled up with water and then it was pumped out. This operation was carried out twice. The first day of our job at Church Farm, it rained – what a mess, but work still had to be done. No Health and Safety rules then. Nor were there any waterproofs supplied. This was a very dangerous job but the Estate staff had always done this kind of work. I was told that some years earlier Reg Child was down a well in Pirton village and they hung the water pump too low over the well and the fumes got in and poor old Reg had to be hauled out of the well semi conscious. The other workmen laid him on the grass until he came round. There were lots of jobs at Croome by which today's laws would not have been allowed to be done, but the workmen had been carrying out these works all their lives and did not know any other ways. Very good and hardworking people and all loyal to the Coventry family.

I remember when I was working at the Vicarage in Earls Croome, installing a Rayburn Cooker, Arthur Seary the bricklayer who was working with us, went down into the cellars and found some bottles of sacramental wine and downed quite a few of them. When Mr Sheppard, the Clerk of Works called, he wanted to know where

Arthur was and, we had to make excuses because he was drunk on the wine. Another time when we were working at Tirley Court, Arthur found a barrel of cider in the cellar which he tasted, and liked, and once again we had to cover up for him during the gaffer's visit. How we got him onto the lorry to come home, I do not know, but they were good times, and you always covered for your mates.

Arthur Seary left and at that time the Estate had taken on a young lad named Brian Overton and his dad, Bill Overton, who was a carpenter, both from Batsford Estate. Brian Overton married a girl named Sheila and they went to live at New Cottages, Wadborough, before that they were living at Severn Bank House in some flats but then Bill Overton and Mrs Overton eventually moved into the house which was vacated by the Searys.

Brian Overton came as lorry driver to the Estate, and there was a new lorry purchased for the building department. After some time being on my own I was put with Brian because there was going to be a big 'do' arranged down at the Temple Greenhouse for Lord Coventry, whether it was his birthday or not I don't know, but we were put on doing the side of the road from Worcester Lodge to the Temple Greenhouse. Brian Overton and myself started on this and it was a monotonous job, although of course part of our work. Some days Brian had to go off and I was left there on my own and we did what we called the siding of the road, cutting the grass back and digging grips for the water to drain off. I also drove the Estate lorry when Brian was away sick. During the winter months, Brian and myself had to deliver lorry loads of logs to several Estate workers' houses, these logs were cut at the Estate forestry yard.

When Bill Overton arrived on the Estate he had an old wagon with glass along the top half which was so dangerous because the glass was plate not safety glass. He had built this vehicle himself. What a death trap it was! Later he had a motorised bike and was never safe on that. One night after finishing work he peddled this thing down the yard and knocked the reflectors off Mr Hartland's Standard car. Another time he went down the yard, couldn't turn at the road and went between the telephone box and the telegraph pole finishing up in No. 8s hedge.

One day we had to do some work at Townstreet Cottages, Tirley, all part of the Estate. At the rear of the four cottages the ground came up to the kitchen window sills, so it was decided that this ground was to be dug out about four feet, a new concrete block retaining wall built and the ground concreted between wall and cottages. The cottages were up a steep bank from the road. Everything had to be done by hand, the excavating, hauling the concrete blocks – you had to have two men on a wheelbarrow, one with a rope over his shoulder on to the handles, then one with a rope tied to the front for pulling. I mixed all the concrete for this job but I still had to help with the barrowing. Happy days?

Another day we were working at Naunton smallholding and I was mixing concrete in the Parker mixer, near the fence, when work was stopped because of the discovery of a wasps' nest. Harry Baker, the bricklayer, said he could soon deal with the nest by pouring petrol over it, which he did, but in so doing he burnt the fencing down. Luckily we rescued the mixer. Another time, working at the same place, we were digging out a new septic tank but due to ground conditions, the water course, the hole got bigger and bigger. Mr Sheppard ordered some rapid hardening cement and this was put in by the bag in the base of the excavation and it steamed up like a sauna. Because of this we used some new liquid which again was meant to be quick setting but, alas, Sid Clifford, who was my mate working in the hole, got covered when Tom Sherwood unfortunately spilt some over the edge of the excavations. This resulted in some very nasty words and Sid getting some of his hair burnt off. We eventually secured the hole and building work started the next day.

Whilst putting in the new flood bolts down at Severn Stoke for which the estate was responsible, we had to use a ladder to get into the deep ditch. You can imagine what happened when the oil tankers came up the Severn. The water was first sucked out and after they had gone would rush up the ditches. I'm sorry to say that one time the men didn't tell Bill Overton about this when he was working in the ditch. Poor old Bill got a real soaking. Bill Overton was an accident waiting to happen, he never looked for problems, but when he was with you on site you just had to make sure things were okay. He used to wear thick glasses and I'm sure he couldn't see properly. With this sort of thing happening, life was never dull.

Townstreet Farm, Tirley was an Estate farm owned by Croome Estate Trustees. When I was working with Fred Gerrard back in the fifties we had to carry out some work to a building which supplied water to the farm. The building was above ground, built of brick with a concrete flat roof. The internal walls were rendered. To the side of the building were some wind sails. When the wind was blowing, the sails would turn and water from a borehole would be pumped inside the holding tank. Our job was to render the inside of the tank. Firstly the sails had to be stopped from turning, then we had to get inside the tank through a covered manhole on the top by lowering a ladder inside. The first job was to hack off the defective render and get the waste outside. We mixed up some new sand and cement render mix with a waterproof powder called Pudlo. Fred and I started putting this on the walls and when it was completed we were taken from the site to let the cement dry out. After two to three weeks we had to return and apply Synthaprufe, a brown liquid, to the walls. It had a horrible smell and we could not stop in the tank for too long at one time, having to get out and have some fresh air. There were no masks or Health & Safety rules at that time. It was an awful job but it had to be done, it's a wonder it did not kill us both. The smell of Synthaprufe was so terrible that we finished up by tying hankies round our faces.

I remember a man being killed on the High Green side of the Iron Bridge. A contractor's lorry working at Defford RAF Camp during demolition work was travelling towards High Green at about 5.15pm when it overturned into a field. The man killed was a workman travelling in the back of the lorry, he had been standing up, holding on to the lorry's ladder rack. When the lorry rolled over he was pinned to the ground by the gantry and the driver couldn't lift the weight off him and unfortunately he died. By the time the fire engine arrived from Upton upon Severn it was too late to save him. This was in the late fifties, maybe 1956 or 1957. We were just biking home from a job at Wadborough, it was a sad end to a day's work.

Before JCB diggers were invented, all septic tank holes and drain trenches were dug by hand. Each labourer was supplied with a plate that was fitted under your shoe to prevent the spade cutting into your shoes or boot (I still have my plate). I have helped dig out many septic tank holes and trenches for the drain pipes, and it was a very tough job. When the hole was dug, the bottom of the tank was concreted, and left for a couple of days to set. The block work was then started, and at the same time the trenches were started in which to lay the glazed stoneware pipes. there were no plastic drainage pipes as yet. Once the blockwork was up to ground level some corrugated galvanised sheeting would be laid over the top with galvanised tubes cut to length to support it. Sometimes props would have to be put inside the tank. Then holes were cut in the tin to insert the manhole covers. First you had to make some framework up. Once everything was ready, the concrete would be mixed by hand and laid on top of the tin and reinforcing rods set in the concrete. It was a very long process, but that was how it was done in those days.

The biggest job we had was at Tirley Court, near Deerhurst Priory, I was working with Sid. We also did a big job on Ron Chipps' farm, Sermans Farm. We took the end out of his house, which I never thought we would be able do on our own, but Sid had the knowledge, and we took all the walls out of the one gable end. He propped everything up with Acrow Props and the end of the house was open although sheeted up at night. It was all rebuilt and Sid did all the bricklaying, plastering and also the plumbing. I was happy to work with him and we got on very well together. I never took any time off work, I was more interested in my job.

In the 1950s when I was working with Sid Clifford, Mr Sheppard, the then Clerk of Works asked if some of us would like a few hours overtime at night, straight after our normal day ended at 5 pm. The work involved clearing some of the items out of the ex-War Department Police huts down on the Croome Road. The items we had to remove were electric light switches complete with centre light cables and lamp shades, baths, basins and toilet pans, and also some good thick lino which had been used on the floors and bench tops. We spent several nights doing this work and loading the items onto the Estate lorry which was driven by Brian Overton. The items were then conveyed to a black and white cottage adjacent to the stables at Severn Bank House. A lot of these items, baths and such like, were in time cleaned up and used in cottage improvements on the Estate. I know for a fact that some bakelite electric light switches were used in the Estate Offices at High Green during improvement works. The overtime pay was at flat rate but it was a bit of extra money in our pay packets and most welcome.

Millpond Farm.

During the late 1950s, Sid Clifford, Fred Gerrard, myself and another labourer were working on the above named farm building a dairy unit. The ground had to be levelled, trenches dug for the footings for the new concrete block walls, and all the concrete was mixed by hand using a mini giant concrete mixer (Parker). Once the concrete was set, the laying of concrete blocks was started. When these were up to the dampcourse level the internal floors were concreted and screeded off. Blockwork was then started again and window and door frames fitted. Steel trusses, which were second hand and originally from Defford RAF camp, had been stored at the Hospital site at Croome for some time. On the Estate we had an old tractor with a front loader fixed to it, probably one of the first front loaders made, with lots of metal work. To climb into the driver's seat you had to make your way through the metalwork which never looked safe. Anyway, the trusses were loaded and brought to site, lifted off trailer and put on the outer walls of the new building. They were then made stable with long planks until they could be fitted into the blockwork with large rawlbolts. The top course of blocks were hollow so you would put the rawlbolts through the angle cleats which were already fitted to the trusses, and concreted into the blocks. Although the first two trusses were lifted and put into position, it was the lifting of the third roof truss which did not go to plan. I was standing on a nine inch block partition wall instructing the tractor driver as to when he should lower the truss onto the wall. The truss was placed on the external walls and I had to unhitch the chain that was holding it. That done, the tractor moved away but before the planks could be fixed into position to hold the truss, it started moving towards me. I couldn't get out of its way and I was knocked off the partition wall which was eight feet high. I fell onto the concrete floor below and on my way down the truss caught the finger on my right hand and broke the tendons. Other than that I was a bit shaken up but more concerned about my finger, especially because I played in goal for our local village football team. As there were no vehicles on site the farmer had to phone the Estate office. Mr Sheppard, the Clerk of Works, came and took me to Pershore Cottage Hospital where a metal splint was put on my finger and bandaged up. They also cleaned up my arms where I had fallen against the concrete block. Mr Sheppard then took me home to Pirton. I was off work for three weeks. Mr Eastment got me to fill in a form for "Industrial Accident". Then I had to go to Birmingham for a Medical. My compensation was £35.00. What would I have been awarded today? Anyway, I started back to work

Malcolm Walford attending the Medical Board in Birmingham in 1956

and started playing soccer again, still in goal. My finger is still bent, but it never bothers me. The fall could have been worse. The building is still there and I think back to those times when I go past. All the men I worked with on that site have passed away.

In 1958 I was with Sid Clifford again, working at Severn Bank House. We were preparing the large base for the double garages at the rear of the house, the weather was terribly cold and there were snow showers. We had received the sad news of the awful tragedy which had befallen Manchester United Football Club and that the 'Busby Babes' and news reporters had been killed in an aircrash at Munich. No one felt like working when that news came through, but we had to, so started getting the concrete base down. The timber frames for the garages had been made by the Forestry Department and came in sections with weatherboard cladding. Over the next few days the concrete was mixed and laid the rawlbolts set into the concrete to which we would secure the frame. We then fixed the frame, fitted the weatherboard, leaving only the door to be fitted by the Estate Carpenters. Once completed the whole thing was creosoted. The garages were for the two flats which had been made over the old kitchen area of Severn Bank House.

The weather was still bitterly cold but you had to work in it. We used to use empty forty gallon oil drums, knock some holes in them with a pick and light a roaring fire inside them. There was plenty of wood in the woods at Severn Bank House we could use for our fire.

Holyoak Farm, Upton Snodsbury, farmed by Mr Tarran

During the 1950s a new foul water drain for the farm had to be dug to join up to the main Council sewer. Fortunately, JCB diggers were now around and one was employed to carry out the excavation work. The trench ran from the farmhouse, through the farm yard and across two fields. When the trench was excavated, manhole inspection pits had to be built and four inch glazed stoneware pipes had to be laid. I think there were three bricklayers on site, complete with their labourers. The manholes were built up to a certain height, and then we had to start laying the drainage pipes. These pipes were stood on their ends with the collar down, and the labourers had to cut drainers yarn to length and fit it very tightly to the spigot end. After several cuts with your knife, the blade went blunt and had to be sharpened with a flat stone which was kept in your pocket. The pipe was then handed to the mate in the trench who would push the end of the pipe into the collared end of the one already in place and that pipe had to fit very tightly. Once about twenty pipes had been laid, that is the distance between two manholes, the labourers would mix sand and cement to fill the gap in the collar. This would then be left to set for two to three days. During this time, more pipes would be laid. This job, called caulking, would make your hands very sore. When the first lot of pipes were completed and the cement had set, a rubber plug would be put in both manholes and the stretch of pipework filled with water. If the cement in the collar got damp through a leak, all defective joints had to be cut out and work started all over again. When a couple of lengths had been tested, and no leaks detected, the Clerk of Works was told, so he could inform the Council who would send a man to visit and check the site. They would then, if all went well, allow you to back fill the lengths of drain which had been passed. This was a back breaking job, but it was the only way to do it. In time these works were completed and drainage was connected to the main sewer.

Facilities were not good in those days. There was an old metal canopy under which you sat for meal breaks, nowhere to wash your hands, no proper toilets, and if it was cold, nowhere to warm your hands or body – not very good. Today the manhole chambers are bought ready made, the pipes are plastic and come in long lengths and the collars just have to be banged on. I don't think the Council man even has to come on site to inspect any more.

During the early 1950s there were four work gangs set up:

Gang 1 – Sid Clifford, Brian Hyatt and myself

Gang 2 – Fred Gerrard, Graham Saunders and Reg Child

Gang 3 – Harry Baker and Ern Sherwood

Gang 4 – Herbert Page and Tom Sherwood

Each gang had a set of builders' tools and included were Tilley lamps for working inside properties during the winter months. To prepare to light these lamps you had to make sure they had paraffin, and you also had a small bottle of meths in which you held a small tool which when soaked, you clipped to the stem of the light below the mantle (which was easily broken). Before you lit the lamp you had to pump some pressure in to the vessel then light it. It popped as it started, and the longer it was alight, the more you had to return and pump more pressure in. They were awful lights and they would hiss all the time. It was not very comfortable working in a confined space. When you wanted the light to go out you undid a screw and let all the air out of the vessel. It was the labourers' job to make sure that paraffin and meths, were always on site and also that the globe of the lamp was clean.

During this time with Sid, he started having days off and I didn't know at the time, but there was a disagreement between him and Mr Sheppard. Sid was made foreman at this time, and I was still working with him. We had an apprentice bricklayer with us, a lad called Brian Hyatt who came from Upton-upon-Severn and I would be at work some days but Sid would not turn up. He moved into another house at High Green, No. 6, where he did all the work himself, put a new staircase in and did all the carpentry, but it didn't last very long before he was having more time off and things weren't going well with Mr Sheppard. Eventually I was told one day that Sid

Clifford was leaving.

With this happening, I was put back with Fred Gerrard who had another apprentice with him called Graham Saunders. The first day I started back with Fred, the year would be 1958, we started work on the conversion at Allesborough Farm, top of Pershore bank. I was with Fred for some years from then.

Although Sid had left the Estate as an employee, he was still living at No. 6 High Green, for a couple or three months, before he found another job. I think the best years for me on the Estate were when I was working with Sid Clifford, he was a brilliant tradesman. He could do both bricklaying and carpentry. We carried out a lot of work and were the No.1 gang and undertook major works at Townstreet Cottages, Tirley, and also at Tirley Court Farm in Gloucestershire. During our dinner time, from 1 pm to 1.40 pm, we used to play football in the orchard, but were always back at work on time. Sid and I built the septic tank at High Green Estate Offices. It was a busy time for me labouring for Sid as he was a very fast and good bricklayer. It was great working with him.

Another time when I was with Fred Gerrard and Graham Saunders we were working out at Lower Walcot Farm. The contractors had put up a new concrete framed building and it was then up to us to get the floor concreted. We had a wooden site hut on the job which we called Hut 29. One day Graham was asked to start a fire so that we could boil a kettle. He had some trouble starting the fire so he got the two gallon petrol can and splashed some on the fire and the flames leapt up to the spout of the can. Graham then attempted to kick the can over which he did and set fire to our site hut. Fred and I were quickly there and put the fire out, a very lucky escape because the site hut was near to a lot of farm buildings!

In 1959/60 Lord Coventry's mother had a dairy herd at Earls Croome Court and we, the Building Department of the Estate, were detailed with the works of convering the old cowsheds. Workers including myself, Fred Gerrard and Graham Saunders and others were also on site. Our first job was to start work on the old cow shed hacking off the old render to the walls. During this time a new concrete framed building was erected in the yard, between the black and white barn and the existing cowsheds. Once this building was completed, we had to concrete the internal floors, this was carried out with large loads of gravel with the cement mixer set nearby. I myself, mixed all the concrete and the others labourers wheeled it to where needed, there was no Readymix then. We formed new calf pens, built a new bull pen and also built a concrete ramp for the milk churns. Fred Gerrard and I then built a new concrete manger and all the concrete block walls. Graham Saunders was the apprentice bricklayer and he also helped with the blockwork. In January 2011 I saw the removal of this concrete framed building and demolition of the concrete block walls which we had built. I stood and thought of all the hours we had spent working very hard during that time and it was now all being pulled apart.

During the Nuns' time at Croome Court, they employed their own maintenance staff and also outside contractors such as Colin & Godfrey from Tewkesbury. Some of the staff names I remember – Mr Albert Edwards, Mr Boughton, Mr Johnson, also another Johnson (Bert) and my father, Len Walford, part time and there were others, but I cannot remember all their names. When my father retired from Railway Service, he took on the job of gardener at Croome Court.

I have worked on nearly every house and farm on the Croome Estate during my early years before going into the Clerk of Works office in 1961. I kept a day to day diary (in old exercise books I used to buy from Woolworth's) and made a note of every property I worked on and every bit of work we did.

There were several properties I dreaded going to. The first was Croome Hunt Kennels where you would see all the dead animals which had been collected from the farms. horses, cows, sheep, you name it, it was there. The only building which was worse was called the 'flesh house' where they used to cut up the animals. The second property I hated working at was Baughton Hill Farm. Lovely people the Harbers were, but the farm was very untidy and not a nice place in which to eat your food in the old buildings during meal breaks. The third property was Millpond Farm. Here again, wonderful people the Gerrards, but not a good place for eating on your breaks. This would have been in the 1950s, no Health & Safety then. No site huts to sit in, no fires to sit by in winter. In comparison workers have got it made today in the building industry. Site huts have to be provided, complete with toilets and somewhere to wash your hands, and they even provide you with waterproofs. I know that we used to wash our hands in the cattle trough and dry them as best we could. If it was cold we used to get in the Dutch barn between the bales of hay. Some days when it was very cold, we used to stand up and have a quick sandwich, have a cup of tea from our flask and get back to work. Don't forget we had to bike to and from work in those days, no vans on the Estate at this time. Still the old workforce knew no other way of life and took it in their stride, but it certainly opened my eyes in the early days.

My Family Life

I got married on my twenty first birthday, 14 August 1954, at St. Matthias' Church, Malvern Link, to Mary Pauline Perks. Mary and I had worked together on Defford Aerodrome. One of my jobs was to cycle to the canteen down the Croome Road to collect jugs of tea for the office staff. She worked in the Canteen for the Ministry of Supply and that is how we met. Mary caught my eye straight away, we got talking and I knew quite quickly that we were meant for each other and eventually we got together. There was me in my RAF Battledress top and RAF beret, who could resist me! She was cashier and used to check the tills and I looked forward to my daily visits. Mary was from Malvern Link and some days she would cycle to work and others she would catch the Ministry coach. We met up at the RAF Dance held in the dance hall near to London Arch but I could not really talk to her as she was well protected by her sisters Ella and Edith. At this time Mary was only about fifteen years old.

Eventually I did get to take her out and went and visited her parents at 47 Tanhouse Lane, Malvern Link. Mary and I were both young and very much in love. Some weekends she would come to stay at my parents home at Rose Cottage, sleeping in my room, while I slept on the couch. We got engaged early 1954 and later that year we were married.

After our wedding, we went to live with my Mum and Dad at Rose Cottage. It wasn't an ideal situation. We had only got a little bedroom, a three-quarter bed and we had to live there until a house became empty on the Estate which I could then put in for.

Mary was still working at RAF Defford when we married, but once the airfield closed down, she got a job on the land – a job she had never been used to. A cottage became available at Pirton and we were able to move in. The row of cottages was called Post Office Cottages and we moved into No. 36, the middle one of three. Our cottage used to be the Post Office, which is how these cottages got their name. They were originally for the staff at Pirton Court, but with Pirton Court no longer being a Coventry home, they were handed back to the Estate, for their work people. When Lady Peggy passed away at Pirton Court, the house was then rented to Mr Jack Bayliss. There used to be a post box in the front wall of our house which meant people were walking right in front of our sitting room window, so some time after we moved in, I requested that it be moved.

We could come in from either end of the run of three cottages, if coming from Pirton village, you came in past where Mr & Mrs Adams lived, or if from Pirton Court end, then you would pass where Mr & Mrs Seary lived. Mr Seary was a bricklayer on the Estate, an Irishman and he was married to a girl who used to live at Park Farm cottages, one of the Edwards' girls, and they were already in their cottage when we moved in.

The wages on the Estate were not very good, so we could not afford much furniture. My dad bought us a second-hand cast iron mangle on wheels, with large rollers. I think it cost half a crown (twelve and a half pence today). Another thing he bought us was an axe for me to chop wood for the cottage fires and for burning under the copper in the wash house. I bought some second hand cupboards to put in the kitchen with no doors on, so Mary put some curtains across the front of them. At the time we could not afford to have furniture for the sitting room, so it was only the small kitchen table and two metal chairs. We bought a double bed on hire purchase and some bedroom cupboards, but we couldn't afford a staircarpet. We had a small Rippingdale paraffin stove with one ring and Mary used to cook on the Claco fire grate in the corner of the kitchen. We had a large larder with a stone slab in it. The lighting was provided by a double burner Aladdin paraffin lamp which was horrible to read by. In time we had the front room painted. The existing paintwork was a horrible 'Croome' brown and it took a lot of paint to cover over. Once we got this done we white emulsioned the ceiling and the walls.

Opposite Pirton School there were some very old cottages belonging to the Estate which were going to be demolished at some stage. One of the cottages had a small building nearby with a thatched roof. I enquired of the then Clerk of Works, Mr Ken Sheppard, if I could have the firewood if I pulled the building down for nothing. Mr Sheppard agreed to this and also said I could borrow the tractor and trailer. I thought it would not take me long to pull this building down, load the old thatch and dump it nearby, then load the old wood and take it home to Post Office Cottages. The two large doors were to be salvaged for use on other Estate properties. I made the biggest mistake of my life suggesting I pull this building down, the main problem being with the thatched roof – when I started to strip it, I discovered it was full of pegs which the thatcher had used to hold the thatch in place, and the thatch was also very thick, rotten and wet. I had a hell of a job on my own doing this work and wished I had never bothered with the building. I think, after several weekends and some nights, I eventually got the wood I was after and it kept our old sitting room fire going for some months – but I never volunteered to demolish another building of this type again – not on my own!

Not long after I joined the Estate, I was asked by the then sub-agent Mr H K Eastment, if I would like some overtime on a Saturday morning. There was to be a Fete with side-shows and bowling for the pig at Pirton Court, and was asked if I would mow the lawns. The Estate had purchased a brand new eighteen inch Atco mower with a pedal start and Mr Eastment said he would come and show me how to use it. On the Saturday morning, I reported to Pirton Court from my home just round the corner and met up with Mr Eastment and the new mower. "Come over here Walford", (no christian names then) "and I will show you how to work the mower". He started it up, put the bar across to put it in gear, and shot straight up into the bushes – I couldn't laugh could I? Anyway, we got the machine out of the undergrowth and cleaned it down and I was left to mow the lawns. The Fete started at 2pm and it was a great success. Some years later (in the 1970s) George Kingdon, then Clerk of Works, said that there was an old mower in one of the garages which didn't work. Would I like to take it home to No. 8 High Green where I was then living? This turned out to be that same mower, my son Kevin got it working and used it for several years.

Mrs Clift at Pirton Church Farm, which was adjacent to Pirton Church, was looking for someone to do a spot of gardening. Well I volunteered and the pay was half-a-crown an hour (twelve and a half pence today) and it was not easy! The stinging nettles near the chicken pens were four feet high and cutting these back with a bill hook was no easy task and I got stung many times. When it came to treating her rose bushes you had to apply the treatment with a one inch paint brush, no sprayers were allowed. The money at the end of the week, for three nights working for two hours each was fifteen shillings in total (seventy five pence today). This job did not last very long as Mrs Clift was always behind me saying not to cut this down, and to leave that. In the end I called it a day. With this extra bit of money we bought coal for our grate, coal was then three shillings and sixpence (seventeen and a half pence today) per hundredweight. At this time there was no overtime work on the Estate. No-one knew any different, this was 1956. Mary and I were very happy, we had only been married two years, we were young and did not know what was in front for us. Eventually we got our furniture and made the house quite comfortable.

We also had a wireless, which had acid accumulators in it and a very large battery. Every so often we had to get new batteries and I had to take the accumulator to the garage at Severn Stoke to get it recharged. We had no electricity supply then, and no mains water, the only water was from the pump. There were no flush toilets, only the bucket type. The biggest problem living in the centre cottage was that I had to get up very early and dig a hole in the garden, empty the contents, and back fill the hole, not a very nice job! The water pump was some way from the cottage and I used to fill a large enamel bucket up in the morning and store it under the white Belfast sink. I would also fetch one at night. Eventually electric power finally came, and that was a blessing!

When Mary did the washing, we had to fetch quite a few buckets of water from the pump to fill the large copper in the wash house. Then we had to lay the fire grate with wood and get a good fire going to start the water boiling. Mary had a hard life living as we did, especially as she had come from Malvern Link and was used to the mod. cons. of the day at her parents' home. It must have been quite a shock to Mary's system coming to live in the country, but we were both young and very much in love. At night Mary would sit knitting and I would be outside sawing wood for the open fire in the kitchen.

One of my duties when I first got married and was living at Post Office Cottages which was near Pirton Pool, took place whenever the pool froze over. It was to secure a large notice board with a money box attached, with a padlock and key belonging to the Estate, to the gate opposite Mr & Mrs Corbett's cottage. The notice board read **DONATIONS FOR CROOME D'ABITOT CHURCH.** Once the ice was thick enough for skating, you were allowed to skate on the pool if you made a donation. It was then my job to empty the box last thing at night. In this day and age I do not think the money box would be intact for very long.

We moved into this cottage in about 1955 and when the Seary's moved, a Mr Overton came to live in the end cottage. The Overtons lived there for a few years and then they put in for a house which became empty at Kinnersley, No. 34. Things were improving and when we could afford it, we bought some furniture on hire purchase and also a carpet. After the electric came it was followed by the water supply, but still no flush toilet!

By this time Sid Clifford and I had put in a garage foundation and done the brickwork at No. 37 Post Office Cottages. The garage was made in sections by the forestry department and then erected on site complete with garage doors made by the building department, so I asked the Agent if there was any possibility of my moving house. In early 1958 we moved to the end cottage No. 37. By this time my dad had bought a Ford Popular and the car was kept here.

When our son Kevin was born in May 1958, Mary gave up working on the land. We had to get a cot and baby clothes. Mary's sisters were very good and bought us quite a lot. In September 1960 our daughter Caroline was born. By this time we had got some better furniture for the kitchen and even had the two small bedrooms wallpapered for Kevin and Caroline. My mum and dad were still alive and living in Rose Cottage, with my brother.

Once things had settled down, Mary started looking for a job again. A new school had been built at Severn Stoke and Mary applied for the Cook Supervisor's job, and although she did not get this, she was made second in charge and eventually, when the Head Cook left, she was promoted and stayed at the school for some years. Out of the blue one day, a supervisor from the Council called and spoke to Mary about a job at The Holy Redeemer School in Pershore, it would give her more authority and there were several staff to look after. She applied for and got the job. They not only prepared food for the school in Pershore, but also for Elmley Castle school. She was very well respected and when she changed the menus and added new puddings, more pupils stayed at school for their lunch. The next thing we needed to do, as Mary could not drive, was to sort out some transport for her. We purchased a new Honda 50 scooter from Bladders in Worcester and after several lessons she took the plunge and drove to Pershore. She loved that bike, loved her job, and loved cooking. After several years at Pershore, Mary had a back problem and had to part company with the school. She started making birthday cakes from home, but after someone shopped her for working from home, she had to give this up and carried on looking after the home and supporting me in my work where she could. When Mr Sobey was at Croome Court and running Manpower Services, they got to know that my wife was a cook and she was asked to interview for the post of Catering Manager.

She was accepted for the post and all went well until Mr Sobey started cutting down on the amount of food the boys were given which did not go down well with Mary and they parted company. Sadly Mary's back complaint never improved and she was eventually crippled and was not able to work again. She was a very brave lady and looked after our family well.

In 1961 I passed my driving test and used to go to work in Dad's Ford Popular. I was still playing in goal for Stonehall at this time, and we were still changing at The Fruiterers Arms.

At this time the schoolhouse at Pirton came empty. I was still working with Sid Clifford and works were to be undertaken with other tradesmen and labourers off the Estate, at this property. This was good news for me, because it was not far from home and I could get there at lunchtime. Firstly a JCB was brought in to excavate the hole ready for building a new septic tank. While the bricklayers were building the tank it was up to the labourers to excavate the drain trenches by hand back to the house ready for the glazed stone pipework to be laid. We also had to remove the large wooden partitions which separated both classrooms. These were removed from site by the Estate lorry driver, Brian Overton, and taken to the Hospital site at Croome for storage and eventually they were sold. We then took up several floorboards and excavated and concreted new footings. In place of the wooden partition we built a solid nine inch brick wall complete with chimney flue and chimney stack and fitted a modern, tiled surround, fireplace. The original school bell was taken down off scaffolding we had erected. Where the bell had been we knocked out the brickwork and fitted a new window to allow more light to the main staircase. The glass was cut and I fitted it. All jobs were completed and the site was cleared. Some years before that, Sid Clifford and I and the carpenters had altered the old classrooms into living accommodation. I took the existing bell down from the schoolhouse, which my father used to ring as he always got to school first, walking from Pirton Sidings, and was the one detailed to ring the bell. (That bell is now in my possession and I have had it cleaned.) In September 1961 I got promotion into the office and had several pay rises which helped us a lot.

The School House had not been used for some years but in early 1961 we were on the move again – into Pirton School House. This had everything. Flush toilets and a bathroom, it was heaven. It was a very large house with an equally large garden. Part of the garden had been the old school playground. We had a Rayburn cooker in the kitchen and an open fire in the front room. We were very happy living there.

George Kingdon gave me some hints on decorating and on wallpapering, and I got the bug. I asked if I could have a couple of days off out of my holidays, and he let me have them. I started papering the bedrooms, and then decorated the bathrooms. Next it was time to do the garden, the old children's toilets I made into a nice workshop and the old playground I put down as lawn. Living at Mount Pleasant, in Pirton, at that time was my uncle Bob, with Norman, Phyllis and the twins, Mary and Betty. Uncle Bob used to walk down to us in the evening and spend time with Mary and myself and the kiddies. He thought a lot of my kiddies.

In 1967 I was asked to move into No. 8 High Green. The Estate had just taken on a new general foreman named Alec Corbett who had four children and the house at High Green was not big enough for them. So Mary and I agreed with the Clerk of Works, George Kingdon and we moved to No. 8 High Green. Mary, I and the children loved this house and made it our home. This was a good move as it was nearer the office for my work. Mind you, some days it was too near work, as when men were working late and the works were the other side of the Estate, it paid them to work on, but I still had to see that all was locked up and safe. But that was my job so I had no complaints.

By this time my parents and brother had moved from Wadborough into another Estate cottage at Pirton, it was one of the cottages Mary and I had when we married in 1954. The cottage at Wadborough was being sold, hence my parents had to move.

We had some wonderful times at High Green, but also some sad ones. The saddest day of my life was when I handed the house back to the Estate when Mary and I parted. I have never forgiven myself for the hurt I caused but you cannot turn the clock back. No. 8 High Green was, and always will be, home.

When we moved into No. 8 High Green, Mary was employed by the Nuns who were at Croome Court in the Sewing Room, along with others from High Green village. Some names I can remember are Mabel Compton, Mrs Earle, Mrs Heath, Mrs Cook, Mrs Garrard, Mrs Jones and Mrs Tustin. Their job was to repair the boys' clothes. Mary used to walk down Westfield Lane, through Boat House Cover to the Court. Mrs Earle was the mother-in-law of the Clerk of Works, Mr Kingdon and lived with them at 25 High Green, which was then the Post Office. There were also women from the village who worked at Besford Court and they were collected for work by a mini bus.

Working in the 1950s

It is so difficult to explain to people what the Estate was like when I first joined. It was like going back into the 1800s. The pace of life was so slow, nothing was done in a hurry, but works were carried out and the building department kept the cottages and farms in repair, although a lot of repairs were just bodging jobs, but work was carried out. We used to have to bike to the jobs when I started. I used to have to tie my shovel, pick and anything else needed that day, to the crossbar of my bike. We usually left High Green at 8 a.m. after having started at 7.30 a.m. and been told where we were to go. So by the time you reached your job, say Dunstall Farm, it would often be 9 a.m. so work did not start until after break time. Then we would have to leave to go home at 4.30 p.m. Fred would bike to Croome and I would go home to Pirton, or Wadborough before I got married. They were long days and at that time we also worked on Saturday mornings.

1953, the year I started on Croome:

Scaffolding – Wooden poles were used for scaffold and tied together with wire ropes, forty gallon drums were filled with sand and the poles were wedged inside.

Bricks – A lorry load of bricks, which generally came at 3,000 at a time, all had to be unloaded by hand. Men were brought off site to assist.

Drains – 3", 4" and 6" land drains also had to be unloaded by hand.

Glass cutting – 6' x 5' sheets of glass were ordered and put into the glass store. A specially adapted bench was made for the cutting of the glass, all unloaded by hand.

Cement – Delivered 6 ton at a time. Some was unloaded at High Green yard into the old stable (now offices), some unloaded at the Hospital site at Croome.

Sand – men had to go to Sandford near Severn Stoke to the Estate quarry with the lorry and load by hand then take it to the building sites. All sites had a 6' x 3' sand sieve. Sand for building gravel saved for making concrete lintels, a very hard job for the labourers.

Septic tanks – no plastic ones at this time. Ground had to be dug with spades and picks and mattocks. Once you had got the hole deep enough, concrete the base by hand and build up the tank with concrete blocks. When blockwork was complete, drain connections were put in and concrete on top. Then start on the drainage (by hand) to the property the tank was going to serve. Another hand job.

Salvage – All second hand items, i.e. gates, doors, etc., were brought back to the yard, all hinges, latches and other goods items were salvaged, put into store for reuse on the Estate.

Croome Hunt Kennels – The work to renew the flesh boilers was carried out by the Estate Building dept. No Health and Safety in those days, no gloves were issued. A very dirty and unpleasant job. Could put you off your sandwiches (it did me for three days).

Cookers – New Rayburn cookers were off-loaded at the Hospital Site Stores. They were off-loaded by using two planks off the delivery lorry and wheeled down using a sack truck. A very dangerous job. (Rayburns weighed about 5 cwt.) No cranes or forklifts available.

Snow sweeping – During the winter months at Croome Church, Earls Croome Court, Levant Lodge, Pirton Court. After snowfall, on all these Estate properties, the lead valley gutters were cleaned out by hand by the Estate Building department. All access to the properties was by pole ladders and in some places a second and third ladder would have to be used to get across the roofs. Wooden shovels were used, not metal. Croome Court also had to be dealt with this way before I joined the Estate.

Wells – All drinking wells to Estate farms and cottages were dealt with by the Building department. An awful job, no waterproofs supplied, but the old Estate workers didn't know anything different. All part of their everyday job – this was one job I did not like, but I had to do it.

High Green was a very quiet peaceful village, in those days. In the offices at that time there was Col. Osbert Smith (Agent), Mr H K Eastment (Sub-agent) a woman secretary and the Estate Clerk Mr V Hartland. Mr W Faithful (Forester) also had an office there. There was no Clerk of Works at this time only a Foreman (gaffer) Mr Partridge, who had a small office inside the plumbing store. There were coal fires in several offices and some old radiators which were heated by a coke burner. There was also a double garage with sliding doors and a loft over. (These doors are now fitted to the double garage next door to the Agent's Office.) The buildings up the yard from the office were another single garage, stables, blacksmith and wheelwright shops. The joiners' workshop with old buildings at the back which were used to house all the timber in. At the west end of the joiners' shop there was an old sawmill and some outside bucket type toilets plus an old building which housed lots of skirtings, architraves and mouldings.

Nothing on the Estate was thrown away, if rotten old doors came back to the Estate Yard, all the latches, hinges, and any other ironwork which could be salvaged was saved ready for re-use. All second hand bricks were cleaned and neatly stacked, old cast iron guttering and fittings were checked – if any were good they were placed in the store, cleaned down and painted when it was a wet day, so the men could be kept busy. Galvanised corrugated roof sheeting was saved as were any second hand roof timbers. As the Estate was so large, with many cottages and farms, salvaged materials were regularly used.

In the 1950s the Estate had it's own sand store at Lower Sandford. The labourers off the Estate (including me) had to go with the lorry driver to load whatever sand was required for whichever site we were working on. Once loaded, we would drive to the site and shovel it off – no tipper wagon. All the building gangs on the Estate were issued with a sand sieve approx. 6' x 3', and it was the labourers job to sieve the sand when it was unloaded. What a job this was. If the sand was very wet I used to throw a couple of shovels of cement into it to help it through the sieve, and then the bricklayer was set up for bricklaying. The gravel which fell off the sieve (sandscreen) was used for making concrete lintels, nothing wasted. It was the labourers job to form the boxing and mix the concrete. No time for playing about on the job, because you still had to keep your mate supplied with cement mix for his bricklaying.

The building department had a handcart for materials for local jobs plus a lorry which they had for so many hours per day, then it had to be returned to the Forestry department. The workmen on the Croome Estate for both the Building Department and Forestry Department were very dedicated to their work for the Coventry family and to the Estate, they were in a class of their own. Quite a few of them, either lived in High Green Village or Croome d'Abitot,

Kinnersley, Severn Stoke, Earls Croome and Pirton All used to cycle to work and meet on the Estate Yard to receive instructions from the Clerk of Works or the Head Forester as to which part of the Estate they would be working on.

A 200 gallon underground Petrol Pump was situated opposite the Estate office. Petrol was used for all the Estate vehicles. This pump was finally removed and the underground tank made safe in the late 70s. At the centre of the Estate Yard was the Coal Store. This coal was for the office open fires and a man was detailed during the winter months to keep these fires alight and topped up. The Coke Store was between the Clerk of Works office and the Foresters office. Again a man was detailed to keep the boiler going to ensure the radiators in the offices were kept warm. This did not include the Clerk of Works office or the Foresters office due to there being no radiators in these. They were each issued with a two bar electric fire which were very quickly turned off when Col. Osbert Smith arrived at the offices. He would visit every morning to see where the men were and what jobs were being undertaken.

The Carpenters/Joiners Workshop used to have four carpenters' workbenches and each had a carpenter employed on it. Albert Gerrard was the senior joiner and it was he who would make all the special mouldings for various houses on the Estate. His bench was to the left as you went through the entrance door. (The door to the rear of the workshop was put in during the major alterations to the Yard in 1969.) The bell on top of the workshop was rung, I was told, when the building used to be an open fronted cart shed (before my time). As I have said elsewhere, horses were used by the forestry department and in the building department in years gone by. The bell was rung to get the draymen to work at 6.30 a.m. in order to prepare their horses for the day's work. The horses were stabled at the Estate Yard. The fox on top of the workshop came off the old sawmill which is now situated behind the carpenters' shop. This fox was made by Tommy Child the Estate blacksmith. The old sawmill used to be across the road on the green opposite the Estate offices. At that time the mill also housed the woodworking machine and the joiners' workshop was altered (before my time). There was always a fire in the big fireplace in the joiners' workshop and one was always lit at lunchtime in the old Mess Room adjoining. Quite a few of the Estate workmen would use this Mess Room during the winter months.

I remember that most Saturday mornings men from the Estate forestry department were employed at Croome Church mowing and generally tidying up the Churchyard. Mr Eastment (25 High Green) the Sub-Agent, was allowed two forestry workers on a Saturday morning to dig his garden, mow his lawn and chop firewood. Mr Faithful (6 High Green) was allowed two forestry workers on a Saturday morning to dig his garden, mow his lawns, chop firewood and clean his car.

The forestry department men were also employed to keep the embankments cut back by the Iron Bridge and the fencing in good order. They would also clean out the glazed stoneware rainwater channels running down the sides of the road.

I remember the Estate workers going to the Court to remove the bell from the roof of the Red Wing. There was no scaffolding then, only long wooden pole ladders, and it was slid down the ladders straight on to the bed of the Estate lorry. From there it was conveyed to the Estate Yard. Sometimes, during heavy snowfall we had to go to Croome Church to clear the lead valley gutters and any blocked rainwater pipes. Fred Gerrard also informed me that when the Coventrys were at Croome Court men would have to clear snow which was hanging off the stone parapets. I can now understand why there were so many long ladders stored at the yard including a very large forty five rung pole ladder!

There were two blacksmiths employed by the Estate when I joined in 1953, a Mr Tom Child and Mr Tom Banks. There was always plenty of work for them to do. The Estate ran its own farms, one at Westfield Farm and one at Earls Croome Court, so a lot of farm machinery was brought to the yard for repair. At the front of the yard just in front of the joiners' shop, were piles of pump barrels. Back at this time many Estate cottages did not have a water supply although most had a well in the garden. Pump barrels were brought in to be repaired. Lots of the time the blacksmiths were making gate hangings, latches and all sorts of gate and door furniture and ironwork. Some days the blacksmiths would have to go out with their soldering tools to repair lead valley gutters and lead rainwater downpipes. Nails and bolts were also turned out in the blacksmith's shop. There were two furnace bellows and two anvils in the shop. Tom Child was a grumpy old man but very good at his job and Tom Banks was just the opposite, always merry and jovial. It was a treat to watch the blacksmiths and the joiners at their work.

Estate Toilets 1953

The toilets for the workmen on the Estate were to the rear of the carpenter's workshop. These toilets were not only used by the building department but also for the workmen of the Estate forestry department. The small wooden building housed two bucket type toilets and one piece of corrugated tin to act as a urinal. The toilets were dealt with on a Saturday morning by Frank Sherwood an Estate forestry worker, not a very nice job. The buckets were emptied by digging a hole in the ground, some lime was then spread over the contents, the buckets were washed out and some strong Elsanol tipped in – if not Elsanol, it would be Jeyes Fluid. Jeyes Fluid was also put down the corrugated sheetings. The Estate office I think, had one gents' toilet and the women secretaries had to use Mr Eastment's ground floor WC at his house at 25 High Green. This was then flushed into a large culvert which runs to the rear of High Green village. This culvert was only supposed to take the rainwater off the roofs of the cottages. The cottages on the other side of the road, numbers 2,4,6 and 8 all had bucket type toilets. I know for a fact that some cottages the same side as No. 25 all had bucket toilets and they too were emptied into the large brick culvert and that was where it stayed. This carried on until all the cottages in High Green had septic tanks built. When the yard was altered in 1969, the vehicle washdown drain was connected to the culvert therefore moving the sewage into a large septic tank on High Green farm ground. All drainage now goes into a proper sewage system.

There used to be some very old buildings in the Yard before the improvements of 1969. I have made a plan of these buildings because otherwise no one will know what the yard and office were like in the 1950s.

At the West End of the yard there was a building for mouldings, architraves and skirting boards and it housed some wonderful timbers. The Old Barn/Sawmill adjoined the joiners' shop at the western end of the yard and was full of old timber props and various rubbish. This like many others was pulled down in 1968/69. The new sawmill was built on the green opposite the Estate Yard before I started working on the Estate. This building is now behind the joiners' shop. It was taken down by Estate staff, all roof sheets numbered and the building re-erected. This made our new timber store, ladder store and storage for many other plant items. I have photos of this building before Croome Estate Builders closed and all plant was sold in 1996.

Once the RAF had finished with the Hospital Site it was handed back to the Estate. The Bomb Blast Shelter was used to store thatching straw in, to be used in time to re-thatch various Estate properties.

During the 1950s, the Hospital site (before I took over) was used as a dumping ground for hardcore etc. I remember working with Fred Gerrard on a new hand concrete block machine which was purchased by the Estate, it was not electrical and all had to be done by hand. Fred and I were the pair to use it and Mr Ken Sheppard was the then Clerk of Works. One Saturday morning Mr Sheppard was getting quite cross – he thought it was an easy process and we were going to make a lot of concrete blocks, but this machine only made two blocks at a time but even this was a problem. Firstly I had to mix the aggregate semi dry, then Fred would fill the moulds. Once the moulds were full, you had to pull down a large weighted handle and keep pressing the mix into the mould, then refill the mould and start all over again. The trouble was that when you came to remove the concrete block from the mould – which you did by pulling up a large lever at the side of the machine – if the mix was too dry and you lifted the block out of the machine, it fell apart. I think the machine was put in a building at the Hospital site and never used again. This machine and also the electric block machine were sold during a large sale at the Hospital site when a lot of surplus materials were auctioned. I still have the sale sheet.

The then Clerk of Works, Mr Ken Sheppard, decided that the ambulance garage and morgue buildings would be ideal to service the Estate lorry and concrete mixers. In the ambulance garage an inspection pit was dug out. A concrete base was put in and the sides and ends were built up in concrete blocks with concrete blocks as steps at one end. Railway sleepers were then cut to length and fitted over the top. At the rear of the garage was the old morgue. This building was then used to repair concrete mixer engines and other plant which required attention. These buildings were part of Defford RAF camp but had not been used by the RAF for some years. These workshops did not last very long. The inspection pit was filled in and the old mixers were scrapped. The doors to the ambulances station are not the original ones, they were beyond repair and a pair of second hand barn doors off the Estate were altered to fill this opening.

The garage was then used by Fred Gerrard to store his apples because Fred used to rent Sandy Orchard off the Estate. Fred also had a cider press and made some lovely cider. Mr Sheppard used to live in the house (Keepers Cottage) between Corner Cottage and Stone Cottage, Croome d'Abitot, not far from the London Arch.

We had a lot of fun working out on various farms, but the fun never interfered with our work, we worked very hard. The men who were married and living in tied cottages on the Estate were always frightened of the bosses. One word out of place and you were asked to leave and vacate your cottage. You were told to keep the garden, hedges and the inside of your cottage tidy, the outside repairs were carried out by the building department at no cost to you. High Green village was a very tidy village with all the hedges trimmed. Unfortunately today a lot of the hedges have been ripped out and hard standings put in for cars, what a change from the early 1950s, but time moves on.

When Col. Osbert Smith gave up being Estate Agent, I think he was already Senior Trustee. A new Agent arrived whose name was Mr Chesterman. As Pirton Court was vacant at the time, Mr Chesterman and his family moved in. He drove a black Austin 16. We, the workmen, did not see a lot of him. Some mornings when we were biking to work we would see him around the farms checking gates etc. but we didn't know why. Col. Osbert was related to the Coventry family and would always visit the Boathouse cover and the surrounding grounds every Sunday afternoon, without fail. He was a wonderful man and looked up to by the Estate tenants and workers. It was a very sad day when he passed away, and his large funeral was attended by all the Estate workers. Those who carried his coffin were Estate workers, some from the building department and some from the forestry department.

The next Agent was Mr David Meyrick.

After Dai Partridge, the foreman left, we had a new Clerk of Works whose name was Ken Sheppard. He too lived at the Old Keepers Cottage at Croome when Dai had vacated the property. The next Clerk of Works was Tom Keith and then George Kingdon (who promoted me in 1961 to Stores Controller). George Kingdon and his family moved into Mr Eastment's house at 25 High Green. Mr Eastment and his wife had moved to a cottage on the Estate at Collets Green, called Woodmans Cottage, Powick.

When the water supply came to various Estate properties, the Estate building staff had to visit those properties and make safe the wells which were no longer used. First of all the top had to be removed to allow a ladder to be put down. Once the ladder was in position an oak timber was placed through the ladder rungs, stopping the ladder from sinking into the mud at the bottom of the well. A workman then descended the ladder equipped with a rope and hacksaw. The rope would be tied around six foot of lead pipe to make it secure and the workman would start cutting through the pipe. The workman at the top of the well would take the strain as it was being cut through and when free, it would be pulled to the top of the well. This was done until all the lead pipe was cleared. The scrap lead would be returned to the Estate yard. Old galvanised piping was then put on top of the well opening, with galvanised corrugated sheeting over, and then three inches of concrete, reinforcing irons and a further three inches of concrete laid on top. In 1959, when George Kingdon arrived, I was put with a carpenter whose name was Bill Overton, Brian Overton's dad.

Croome River Cuckoo Pen Wood

In my early days at Croome there were some large elm trees in this wood and large numbers of herons nests. Due to Dutch Elm Disease quite a few of these trees were felled and I am sorry to say that the herons had to abandon their homes, never to return.

The elms which were cut down on the Estate mostly went for firewood but once the bark was removed from these trees it was seen that the wood of some were not infected and I know of people who got hold of some and made some lovely furniture, so you see this timber could have been worth quite a lot of money, and not just burned.

Croome Estate Forestry Department

The main sawmill was originally on the green opposite the Estate Office and there were garages with curved asbestos roofs. This stored the forestry tractor and various other implements plus the builders' lorry which was stored there at night. There were two men employed in the sawmill and quite a large staff who worked on the forestry department. The Pickle Yard where the large creosote tank was, was adjacent to the forester's house No. 6 High Green. The timber felled was transported by the forestry ex-army wagon with a large trailer attached, the large trees were then unloaded in front of the sawmill and winched onto the large travelling saw rack. The timber was cut to various sizes, some for weatherboarding, the off cuts for logs, and some timbers were prepared for the building department into 4"x 2", 3"x 2", 2"x 2" and any other sizes which were required. When the timber was taken into the forestry yard to be cut down into fence rails or posts, it would have to be prepared, the bark cleaned off by hand, and then loaded into racks on the railway trucks as the forestry yard had a small gauge railway track. The wagons, when loaded, were pushed into the large creosote building. A fire would be lit under the tank and the creosote brought up to the boil, then the racks, when full, would be winched up and lowered into the creosote tank. After two days, the racks were lifted out and drained off. The fence material would be stored in proper size storage piles. The forestry men worked very hard and the creosote work was a very dirty job. They were a great bunch of workmen and I was fortunate to have met them all in my job at Croome

Croome Point to Point Race Meeting

This was always held on Easter Tuesday and workmen on the Estate were given the day off to attend. If you did not attend, then you reported for work. I think my wife and I only ever attended one meeting and that was by invitation of the eleventh Earl of Coventry. In previous times, I used to work as when I was Stores Controller I always had plenty of work to carry out.

The Three Counties Show

Here again, the men were allowed a day off but if you did not attend then you reported for work. The Estate used to hire two coaches when the show was originally held in Gloucestershire. The forestry and the building department wives were also allocated tickets. I remember one year the forestry department had their own stand. Again, I never attended the show until later when it was based permanently in Malvern.

Croome Estate and its Tradesmen

Albert Gerrard – Carpenter/Joiner

This man was from a family who all worked at Croome. He was brilliant at his job. Albert's workbench was on the left hand side of the Joiner's Workshop when you entered. He could make anything and I am sure some of the joinery work in Croome Court would have been repaired by him when necessary. I have seen him make various mouldings for replacement skirting boards, picture rails and also the new window frames for Pirton Court. Albert also made the lead lights for these windows. I have seen him using the lead came and solder. Albert also made all the new joinery work for the agent's office including the oak doors and flooring. He made a desk for me when I was promoted to Stores Controller. His tools, planes, of which he had many, were kept in a large wooden box (which was locked) and kept by the open fire in the joiners' shop. This he used to sit on when it was break time. Albert lost quite a few fingers on a midsaw woodworking machine in the late fifties, but after a few months off, returned to work. Some days he was in pain but he never gave in and was still making special doors until he passed away. A truly good tradesman and very loyal to the Estate.

Fred Gerrard – Bricklayer/Stonemason/Roofer

Fred was a brother to Albert, and again a man who knew his job. He was a very hard worker and worked out in all weathers. He would give one hundred per cent every day. I was put with Fred in late 1953 and worked at various properties around the large Estate. We dug out holes for septic tanks (no JCB then), this was not light work, went down various wells to clean them out, up a forty five rung pole ladder to remove an unsafe chimney pot at Earls Croome Court and carry it back down to the ground, that took some balancing coming down a ladder. Fred would start work as soon as we got on the job at 7.30, only stopping for short meal breaks until we finished at 5 p.m. If we were cycling from work which was usually the case, we would start out a few minutes earlier. Another good, honest worker, loyal to the Estate. Once, when we were at Earls Croome Court, Fred saved the cowman's life from an angry bull which had got out of its pen. Fred was very young when he joined Croome and was called up for the Second World War but he rejoined the Estate at the end of hostilities, and his service to the Estate continued. Quite a lot of the Estate workforce served in the Second World War and some also in the 1914/18 war. Really good characters. I wish I had listened to more of their stories.

Tommy Child and Tom Banks – Blacksmiths

Both of these men were at Croome when I started. I think they had been employed by the Estate for some years. I presume they would have been at the Estate when cart horses were employed, so the shoeing would have been carried out by these two. All the ironworks for works on the Estate were carried out by them, hinges, latches, bolts – you name it, they made it. In front of the new joiner's shop (where the cars park now) was very crowded. There were pump barrels all waiting to be repaired, galvanised water piping, farm implements of all types and quite a lot of salvaged timber. Over the years, you still get pieces of metal coming out of the ground. It was good to see both blacksmiths' bellows working and the sound of their hammers hitting the anvils. Two men good at their trade and loyal to the Estate

Reg Child (son of Tommy Child) – General Handyman

Reg could turn his hand to any job. His dad, Tommy, taught him the blacksmiths' trade and when Tommy and Tom Banks retired, Reg took over the duty of making any metal work which was required on the Estate. Reg also worked out with the gangs, it might be plumbing, putting up new cast iron guttering, lead flashing and wipe lead pipe joints, repair pump barrels and on some days, tractor driving, he would do everything. Reg lived with his dad at Stone Cottage, Croome. His mum passed away some years ago and Reg looked after his dad did all the washing, cooking, cleaning and fetching the shopping from Pershore. Reg didn't have an easy life with his dad. Reg and Frank Tallet took on the job at the Hospital site of making concrete blocks for use on the Estate. Reg mixed the aggregate and barrowed it into the building. Frank raked it into the machine. Reg would also be called on to repair Rayburn cookers of which there were quite a few on the Estate. Sadly Reg passed away only a few weeks before he was due to retire and is buried with his mum and dad in Croome churchyard. Col. Anthony Smith, Senior Trustee, attended Reg's funeral, together with a lot of his workmates, and said at the graveside, "Goodbye old friend" What wonderful words for another loyal employee.

Herbert Page – Bricklayer,
Tom and Ernest Sherwood – General Labourers

Herbert Page was getting on a bit when I joined Croome and so were brothers Tom and Ernest Sherwood. Herbert and Tom worked together and Ernest floated between different tradesmen. You could always tell where Herbert and Tom had been if you had to remove some brickwork or tiling where they had been working, Tom always mixed his mix two sand and one of cement. It would set so hard that we had a lot of trouble knocking their work apart. The biggest problem occured if you came to remove an old fireplace – you could always tell if they had fitted it. Herbert and Tom drove around in an old Austin Seven – never safe but at that time there were not many cars on the road. At one time I have seen Tom, when travelling with Herbert to a job in Kinnersley, open his door and stick his leg out, foot to the ground, to slow the car down! Herbert Page lived at No. 9 High Green, Tom lived and No. 8 and Ernest lived at No. 19. They were all old fashioned Estate workers, worked on the Estate all their lives, never knew anything different and all very loyal.

Croome Estate Workers

Frank Baldwin – Part Time Lorry Driver

Frank would drive the Estate lorry first thing in the mornings to get building materials to various sites. The lorry, although it belonged to the Estate, was from the forestry department. We had it for three hours and then it had to be returned to the forestry department. When Frank finished his driving for the day, he would help with other building works on the Estate.

Billy Brown – Painter

I didn't know much about this man. He lived in one of the Estate cottages at Pirton. We worked together on various properties, mainly Severn Bank House, where we were carrying out a large restoration job. He did not stay at Croome very long. When Mary and I got married in 1954, we moved into the cottage he had vacated.

Charlie Jones – Painter

Charlie started the same day as me. He was one of the original gardeners at Croome Court. He started as a general labourer but was promoted to painter. Charlie was a great man to work with, never a dull moment when you were on a job. We had fun, but always got on with our work. He thought the world of the Coventry family. He too is buried in Croome Churchyard, but I am afraid there is no headstone.

Brian Denslow – Apprentice Carpenter

Worked with Albert Gerrard in the joiner's workshop. Not much known about him.

Brian Finch – Apprentice Carpenter

Also worked under Albert Gerrard in the Workshop. Came out on site on various occasions. He was always full of fun and playing tricks on you. I don't think he made it to carpenter grade.

Dai Partridge (Gaffer)

There was no Clerk of Works when I started at Croome, just a foreman. Dai was an ex Grenadier Guardsman. He used to have a small office in the plumbing store and drove a Ford Popular van. He lived in the Game Keeper's house at Croome, the house between Corner Cottage and Stone Cottage, near the Marble Arch. He used to walk to the office in the mornings, he was not allowed to take the van home. Some mornings I would pick him up on my motorbike when I came from mum and dad's at Pirton Sidings – this was before I was married. Dai did not stop long at Croome and I don't know where he went after.

Arthur Turk – Rough Carpenter (son of Alf Turk)

Arthur was the man for carrying out site works like fixing gate posts and gates, also fencing and sometimes roofing. His father worked for the forestry department in the saw mill at High Green.

Ken Sheppard, Clerk of Works 1950s (lived on the Estate)

Mr Sheppard was a short stocky little fellow. I did not get on with him when he first started but he was the gaffer. I was then working with Fred Gerrard.

Tom Keith, Clerk of Works (lived on the Estate at Croome)

Again I did not have much contact with him. He used to like his drink and some days would lock himself in his office. I always remember the time when he collected Fred Gerrard and myself from a job at Nos. 3 and 4 Allesborough Cottages in the A35 van, because he was drunk as a lord. We left Allesborough and it was very frightening because he kept mounting the grass verge. Fred sat in the front passenger seat and was ready to pull the keys out of the ignition. Fred and I were very glad to get to Corner Cottage Croome where Fred lived and where I had left my pushbike. Mr Keith did not last very long in his job at Croome.

Bill Talbot, Plumber (lived on the Estate)

Bill always arrived for work on an old ladies' pushbike. He was, I was told, a plumber by trade. He eventually made general foreman and took charge when we had no Clerk of Works. He thought he knew everything, but he did not. He was supposed to have sat his Clerk of Works exam with Tom Keith's help, but he did not last long when George Kingdon arrived. Bill left and took a job in the Cotswolds.

David Meyrick, Land Agent (lived at Severn Bank House)

Mr Meyrick arrived, I would think, about 1958. At this time I was still working with Fred Gerrard. We, the workmen, did not see much of the Agents unless they visited the building sites, the farms or cottages, we were working on. When I was promoted to the office in 1961 I got more involved with Mr Meyrick. I thought he was a good man for Croome, very straightforward. He was not liked by all including the Estate farmers, first of all he stopped the farmers having everything for nothing from the Estate stores, so that put him in their bad books straight away, but I found him very straight and fair. If you asked him and he said no, you had no need to ask him again. Yes, I got on very well with him.

George Kingdon, Clerk of Works (lived at 25 High Green)

Mr Kingdon was my boss and came to Croome in 1959. He taught me everything, which helped me a lot, especially when he left and Lord Coventry made the building department into a company. Mr Kingdon always told me to keep a note of things, which I did and they certainly helped me when Lord Coventry took his directors to court (more written about this later on).

Mr Kingdon and I got on very well. We were together in the office for over eighteen years. He was a very good draughtsman and was very loyal to the Estate. Sorry to say he passed away some two years after leaving the Estate. Yes, I owe Mr Kingdon a lot and am grateful for all he taught me.

John Henderson – Land Agent

John came to the Estate in the 1960s. He came as Assistant Agent to David Meyrick and was made Resident Agent when Mr Meyrick left in 1967/8. John and I have know each other for some years and have generally got on well together. During Mr Kingdon's time as Clerk of Works, I did not have much contact with the Agent, but when I was made Manager of Croome Estate Builders in 1986, I had more contact with John. During the 1980s gales, John was in London for the then Sun Alliance Group and could not get back home. So I took charge, with Pip Webster, of the repairs to Estate cottages and farms which had been hit by the gales.

Bob Walford (my uncle) Estate Forester

Uncle Bob completed fifty nine years service on the Estate. It was he who told me there was a job available in the building department on the Croome Estate. So it is uncle Bob I have to thank for all the years I've been at Croome, and the fact that there is now another Walford clocking up more than fifty years of service. He lived at

Pirton Sidings in a black and white thatched house not far from the railway sidings, with his wife Edith, who was a Rimell, sister to Reg Child's mother. We lived not far away at 47 Rose Cottage, Pirton Sidings. When his wife passed away, his daughter Phyllis and her husband Norman Fassnidge came to live with him. They had twins, Betty and Mary, another daughter Margaret and a son Robert. Bob, Norman and Robert worked at some time on the Estate. Bob was very well liked by Col. Osbert Smith. When the black and white cottage was eventually pulled down by the Estate in the 60s, the family moved into Mount Pleasant, Pirton, which I am told was the old headmaster at Severn Stoke School's house. Bob lived at Mount Pleasant until he passed away and was buried at Pirton Church with a full turn out of Estate staff and trustees. He was very popular and well liked, another true Estate worker and loyal employee of the Coventry family and Croome Estate Trustees.

Bill Overton – Carpenter

Lived on the Estate. He followed Ken Sheppard from Batsford Esate. Always good for a laugh.

Brian Overton – Lorry Driver

Son of Bill Overton, he also came from Batsford Estate. Brian also ran the stores at the Estate besides driving the lorry, delivering materials to sites and he used to keep a check on materials. He was offered the storeman's job by Mr Kingdon but did not want it, hence I took the job. Brian also carried out plumbing repairs and was a good all round tradesman. I had some good times on site with Brian and it was he who helped me at night at the Hospital site at Croome to prepare the building for our new stores. Brian, like me, is a very tidy person.

Donald Smith Keitley – Apprentice Carpenter/Joiner

Donald came from Severn Stoke where he lived with his parents, sister and brother. He came on the Estate on a five year apprenticeship and was put with Tom Grinter. Donald turned out to be a very good joiner and he has Tom to thank for teaching him the skills of joinery. Donald and I got on very well and played together for our local football teams, Severn Stoke and Stonehall United. Donald would have gone far in football, he was an outstanding player. Donald left the Estate and went to work elsewhere at the end of his apprenticeship at Croome

Maurice Sherwood – Apprentice Carpenter

Half brother to Donald Smith Keitley. Maurice was put with Bill Overton to learn his trade and although very keen to learn, I don't think he had a good teacher. The Sherwoods go back a long way on the Estate. Maurice' mother lived at Croome Court where she was employed and I think Maurice was born at Croome Court. We had some good times when working on various sites. He left the Estate and went to work for the Air Ministry Police at Tilesford Airfield.

Owen Clayton – Bricklayer

Lived on the Estate 1950s. Good worker. Did not stay long at Croome.

Sid Collins – Handyman

Lived with his mum and dad at the Yorkshire Grey Inn. Worked with Fred Gerrard. Moved onto the Estate in High Green village when he married. Will write more about Sid later.

Chris Yorgens – Carpenter

He joined the Estate when the work force was increased in the

1950s. He lived on the Estate, and was very good at his job. He always polished his shoes before going home at 5 pm.

Harry Baker – Bricklayer
Lived on the Estate in Kinnersley and came on the Estate in the 1950s. Easy to get on with on site, good tradesman. Had some good times together.

Stan Noke – Carpenter
Joined the Estate in the 1950s. Lived in Worcester and push biked to High Green yard every day. Not a bad tradesman. Sadly Stan passed away some years later.

Bill Thomas – Bricklayer
Joined the Estate in the 1950s. Lived in High Green village. Didn't stay long at Croome.

Jim Roach – Handyman
Came to Croome at same time as Bill Thomas. Lived next door to me at Post Office Cottages, Pirton. Thought he knew everything – lazy. Didn't stay long at Croome.

Arthur Seary – Bricklayer
Came to Croome in the 1950s and lived at Post Office Cottages, Pirton. Married to a girl from Marl Bank Cottage by the name of Edwards. Often covered up for him on site when Mr Sheppard came. Got the sack after threatening Mr Sheppard with a knife on site.

Tom Cooling – Labourer
Derek Drew – Labourer } all lived on the Estate
Brian Minette – Labourer

Frank Tallett – Handyman
Lived locally. I think he was laid off by Mr Kingdon but don't know why. Still lives in Kempsey.

Brian Hyatt – Apprentice Bricklayer
Brian lived with his parents in Holly Green, very tough lad. Worked with a bricklayer named Owen Clayton, then with Sid Clifford and myself. Did not finish his apprenticeship.

Sidney Clifford – Bricklayer/Carpenter
Lived at No. 9 High Green at first and moved into No. 6 High Green when it became vacant. Sid arrived on the Estate in 1955 with his family. I was put with Sid and we worked together for quite a few years. A very good tradesman – could turn his hand to any trade. Finally left the Estate after a fall out with Mr Sheppard, Clerk of Works. Sadly Sid passed away some years ago – very much missed.

Graham Saunders – Apprentice Bricklayer
Graham lived with his parents at Ripple where his dad was the local policeman. Came to work with Fred Gerrard and I. Did not finish his apprenticeship.

Clive Johnson – Apprentice Carpenter
Lived with his parents in Severn Stoke. Worked under Albert Gerrard in the joiners' shop, also worked on site. Left Croome to work in the car trade at garage in Kempsey. In 1979 he married my daughter and they now live at Malvern.

Alec Brown – Painter
Another Severn Stoke lad and a very keen fisherman. Good to be with on site. Sadly he passed away with cancer some years ago.

Bill Middleton – Tractor Driver/Labourer

Lived on the Estate at Earls Croome Court Lodge. He came on the Estate in the 1960s. Came from another building firm in Worcester. Bill was a very large built man so he was put to drive the tractor. Did a lot of work on site. Didn't get on very well with the other workmen, as when on piecework, he would not get off the tractor to help unload the trailer. Sadly Bill has now passed away.

Mick Jarvis – General Labourer

Came from Littleworth, near Norton. Only stopped at Croome a couple of years, he couldn't hit it off with Mr Kingdon. Caught poaching rabbits in works time, and left soon after being caught. Sadly passed away some years later.

Billy Wellon – General Labourer

Used to live at Severn Stoke. Moved into High Green village when he started on the Estate in the 1960s. Billy worked on the maintenance staff at Croome Court when the nuns were there and moved onto the Estate when they left. Billy was a good honest worker, could put his hand to anything. In time he bought his house in High Green, left the Estate, but still lives in the village.

Ron Woodyatt – General Labourer

Came on the Estate in the 1960s and moved into an Estate house in Kinnersley. He left the Estate in the 1980s. Due to ill health he and his wife have just moved from Kinnersley to a bungalow in Upton. Good worker. Ran the site at Corse Lawn with Jeff Jenks.

Malcolm Jones – Painter

Another local lad. Came on the Estate and was put with Charlie Jones. They got on well together and Malcolm stayed at Croome for some years. Another good mate to be with on site.

Norman Homer – Painter

Came from the village of Norton, near Worcester, and came to live with his wife in a tied cottage at High Green. Started with Charlie Jones then when Charlie retired, Norman took over his job and Alec Brown was put with Norman. Another good mate also played football with Donald Smith Keitley and I, left the Estate after some years and started up on his own.

Bill Hooper – Carpenter/Handyman

Came to work on the Estate about 1967/68. He lived on the Estate and was an all round man, could turn his hand to anything. Got promoted to foreman at a later date. Sadly Bill passed away some years ago and is buried at Severn Stoke Churchyard, next to his son.

Tom Campion – General Foreman

Came to work on the Estate at Croome about 1967/8 and lived on the Estate at Hemming Field Cottage. Worked under Mr Kingdon. He left and went to work for Wychavon Council as a Building Inspector.

Alex Corbett – General Foreman

He came on the Estate about 1966 and lived with his wife and family in High Green village at first. His wife got a job at either Besford Court or Croome Court when the nuns were there. Alex was good to be with, he worked hard and knew his job. He got on well with Mr Kingdon. They moved into Pirton School when I left to move into No. 8 High Green in 1967. We all used to play darts for the Estate darts team. He finally left Croome because his wife wanted to return to Angus in Scotland where they originally came from.

Tom Grinter – Carpenter

I don't know where Tom came from but was with the Estate for some years, very good at his job and good when out on site working. He lived on the Estate.

Bob Northcott – Carpenter

Came to Croome and worked mostly on sites. Good at his work, got on well with the rest of the workforce.

I also remember the tenant farmer of Pirton Court Farm, Mr Hayden Jenkins, committing suicide by hanging himself in the cowshed opposite the old black and white cottages. He was a wonderful man.

Croome Estate Personnel and Equipment

People I have known at Croome since 1953 to the present date:

AGENTS:
Mr Chesterman
Mr Bellingham
Mr Meyrick
Mr Henderson
Mrs Webster
Mr H K Eastment *(sub-agent)*

ASSISTANT AGENTS:
Mr N Ford
Mr B Hale

SECRETARIES:
Mrs Thornton
Mrs Stuart
Mrs Fothergill
Mrs J Soley
Sarah

ARCHITECTS:
Mr R Coneybeare
Mr T Jones
Mr P Preston

TRUSTEES:
Lt Col Osbert Smith
Lt Col Anthony Smith
Major Rowcliffe
Col. Barker
Peter Pierpoint
Mr Hoare
Mr Beresford
Mr Scott
Mr Shaffer *(Trustee Accountant)*

ESTATE CLERKS:
Mr Hartland
Mr J Reagan
Mr P Morgan
Mr E Grainger
Mr K Freeman
Mr J Taylor
Mr J Hill

ARCHIVIST:
Mrs Jill Tovey

DIRECTORS:
Mr J Jenks
Mr K Hamer
Mrs K Hamer
Mr Len Pinnock

CLERKS OF WORKS:
Mr K Sheppard
Mr T Keith
Mr G Kingdon
Mr M Walford 1986-2009

BRICKLAYERS:
Mr F Gerrard
Mr H Page
Mr A Seary
Mr W Hale
Mr R Currin
Mr S Jeacock
Mr H Baker
Mr S Clifford
Mr B Thomas
Mr D Jenkins
Mr S Collins
Mr P Bull
Mr P Downes
Mr L French

APPRENTICE BRICKLAYERS:
Mr G Saunders
Mr B Hyatt

FOREMEN:
Mr B Talbot
Mr T Campion
Mr A Corbett
Mr S Clifford
Mr Dai Partridge
Mr Sid Collins

CARPENTERS JOINERS:
Mr A Gerrard
Mr T Grinter
Mr C Yorgens
Mr P Lippett
Mr M Taylor
Mr Bill Overton
Mr J Lawton
Mr D Trinder
Mr B Hooper
Mr C Pettifer
Mr J Edwards
Mr R Northcott
Mr A Turk
Mr J Bullett
Mr S Noke

APPRENTICE CARPENTERS:
Mr B Finch
Mr B Denslow
Mr D Smith Keitley
Mr C Johnson
Mr M Sherwood
Mr J Bluck
Mr D Mackenzie

BLACKSMITHS:

Mr T Child

Mr T Banks

Mr R Child

GENERAL LABOURERS/ HANDYMEN:

Mr F Baldwin *(Lorry driver)*

Mr T Sherwood

Mr E Sherwood

Mr D Greenwell

Mr D Drew

Mr B Minette

Mr A Sheward

Mr M Jarvis

Mr F Tallett

Mr K Walford

Mr B Wellon

Mr R Woodyatt

Mr M Poole

Mr G Hartland

Mr J Kirk

Mr K Withers

Mr W Andrews

Mr B Overton *(Lorry driver)*

Mr B Middleton

Mr A Overton

Mr N Milinsic

Mr J Roach

Mr I Wiggett

FORESTRY WORKERS:

Mr A Turk

Mr G Gerrard

Mr J Gerrard

Mr H Espin

Mr A Cook

Mr F Sherwood

Mr D Beale

Mr R Neathway

Mr A Deakin

Mr G Deakin

Mr N Fassnidge

Mr R Fassnidge

Mr L Walford

Mr B Roberts

Mr J Hodson

Mr P Johnson

Mr C Roberts

Mr F Yapp

Mr J Hemming *(Snr)*

Mr J Hemming *(Jnr)*

Mr A Bluck

Mr D Bluck

Mr J Honeybourne

Mr Forester

Mr Kevin Walford

SAWMILL:

Mr T Hayden

Mr G Banks

Mr G Price

FORESTERS:

Mr Faithfull
Mr Goodhead
Mr Teasedale
Mr Reece
Mr Garrard
Mr B Walford

OFFICE STAFF

Mrs C Morgan
Mrs J Bentley
Miss Sue Smith
Miss Jane Perks
Mrs C Hewitt
Mrs K Paul
Mrs Tina Hamer
Mrs G Powell

CLEANERS:

Mrs C Jones
Mrs M Compton
Mrs S Price

PAINTERS:

Mr C Jones
Mr B Brown
Mr Bill Dodkin
Mr N Homer
Mr A Brown
Mr M Jones
Mr J Harris

GAMEKEEPERS:

Mr Albert Bray
Mr G Crook
Mr Gilbert
Mr Clifford
Mr G Proverb
Mr Denley
Mr E Odell
Mr Lindsey

BUILDING INSPECTORS:

Mr Finch	Upton RDC	Water Inspector
Mr Cromwell	Upton RDC	Sanitary Inspector
Mr Warren	Pershore	Sanitary Inspector
Dot Clement	Upton RDC	Rat Catcher

Various other people who have worked for the Estate:

Mr Dick Davies	Westfield Farm Estate
Mr Tom Taylor	Earls Croome Court Farm
Mr Pritchard	Croome Estate Farm Manager
Mr Maxwell	Croome Estate Farm Manager
Mr Bert Johnson	Earls Croome Court Gardens
Mr Paddy Weaver	Earls Croome Court Gardens
Mr Adrian Cook	Earls Croome Court Gardens
Mr & Mrs B Tommy	Staff at Earls Croome Court
Mr & Mrs Wallhead	Staff at Earls Croome Court
Mr & Mrs Callaghan	Staff at Earls Croome Court
Mrs P Williams	Staff at Earls Croome Court
Mrs Margaret Parker	Staff at Earls Croome Court
Mr Jock Adams	Chauffeur at Pirton Court
Mr Harry Corbett	Gardener at Pirton Court

LOCAL PEOPLE:

Mr Derret	Severn Stoke Post Office
Mr C Ashthorpe	Severn Stoke Garage
Mr B Ball	Severn Stoke Postman
Mr Benbow	Severn Stoke Policeman
Mr Knight	Severn Stoke School Headmaster
Mr M Lovell	Kinnersley Blacksmith
Derek & Letty Deveraux	Severn Stoke Rose & Crown
Mr Bates	Severn Stoke Boars Head
Mr G Nichols	Kinnersley The Oak
Mr D Herod	Kinnersley The Oak

BUILDING REPS:

Mr W Tromans	MAC	Bristol
Mr A Jenkins	Western Trading	Gloucester
Mr Peplow	Sharpe & Fisher	Cheltenham
Mr T Jones	W F Bailey	Worcester
Mr Whitehead	W F Bailey	Worcester
Mr Bathe	J R Kent	Gloucester
Mr J Brown	Underwood	Worcester
Mr K Powell	Underwood	Worcester
Mr Freeman	Underwood Steel	Worcester
Mr G Palmer	Underwood	Worcester
Mr Partridge	Rea & Sons	Worcester
Mr T Hill	Rea & Sons	Worcester
Mr Tudge	Worcester Tool & Fix	Worcester
Mr Reece	County Building Supplies	Malvern
Mr Ian Dick	Jewson	Worcester
Mr John Alan	Jewson	Worcester
Mr J Palmer	J F Halls	Worcester
Mr B Mason	Malvern Glass	Malvern
Mr Budd	Chalford Building Supplies	Gloucester

CONTRACTORS:

Bushell & Thomas	Builders
D Miller	Painters
Mr Butler	Scaffolding
Mrs M Jones	Zenith Plant Hire
Mr Cole	Felt Roofing
Hull & Stevenson	Builders
Mr Zeigler	Flooring
Mr C Peck	Electrical
Mick Ormsby	Plumbing

CONTRACTORS (CONTINUED):

TCG Contractors	Painting & Decorating
City Signs	Signage
S Perkins	Heating Engineer
M Grosvenor	Electrics
Mr S Perkins	Scrap Iron
Mr J Thould	Haywards
Mr R Cheese	Haywards
Mr G Willliams	Haywards
Mr T Payne	Haywards
Mr E Fall	Haywards
Bob & Rupert	Haywards

LEVANT LODGE:

Mr E Thompson	Gardens
Mr I Jones	Gardens
Mr B Holland	Gardens
Mr K Walford	Gardens
Mr A Coole	Gardens
Mr B Fitzer	Cowman for Col. O. Smith
Mr G Collins	Gardens
Mr A Biddulph	Gardens
Mr R Powell	Gardens
Mrs G Powell	Gardens

CONTRACTORS TO LEVANT:

Mr Bob Duggan	Gardens
Mr Haydn Ebrey	Gardens
Mr T Whitfield	Mower Repairs
Mr B Luce	Tree Surgeon

Estate Properties I have worked on since 1953:

Sermons Farm, Pirton	Sermons Farm Cottage, Wadborough
Narrow Wood Farm, Wadborough	Narrow Wood Farm Cottages
Hermitage Farm, Wadborough	Hermitage Farm Cottages
Caddicroft Farm, Drakes Broughton	Caddicroft Farm Cottages
Chevington Farm, Drakes Broughton	Broughton Farm, Drakes Broughton
Firs Farm, Drakes Broughton	Walcot Farm, Drakes Broughton
The Lodge, Drakes Broughton	Stone Cottages, Drakes Broughton
Allesborough Farm, Pershore	Allesborough Farm Cottages
Pinvin Smallholding	The Hurst, Wyre Piddle
The Old Jam Factory, Pershore	Coventry Arms, Pinvin
Deerhurst Terrace, Pinvin	Rose Cottage, Pirton Sidings
New Cottages, Pirton	Church Farm, Grafton Flyford
Upton Snodsbury Church	Yew Tree Farm, Upton Snodsbury
Libbery Farm, Upton Snodsbury	The Old Mill, Grafton Flyford
Court Farm, Upton Snodsbury	Church Farm, Pirton
Church Farm Cottages, Pirton	Ramsden Cottages
Elm Farm, Pirton	Pirton House
Pirton School	Swanbrook Farm
Post Office Cottages	Mount Pleasant
Pirton Pool Cottages	Blacksmiths Shop, Pirton
All Estate Cottages at Pirton	Croome Estate Offices
All Estate Cottages at High Green	Coventry Arms, High Green
High Green Farm	Naunton Farm
Naunton Farm Cottages	Naunton Smallholding
Birch Farm	All Cottages, Birch Lane
Boars Head, Severn Stoke	Rose & Crown, Severn Stoke
All Cottages, Severn Stoke	Severn Stoke Church
All Cottages at Birch Green	Chevington Lodge
Clifton Court Farm	Clifton Court Farm Cottages
Lower Farm Clifton	Lower Farm Clifton Cottages

Holy Oak Farm	Holy Oak Farm Cottages
Croome Church	Keepers Cottage, Croome
Corner Cottage, Croome	Stone Cottage, Croome
Old Slaughter House, Croome	Flower Garden Cottage, Croome
Iron Bridge, Croome	London Lodge, Croome
Marble Arch, Croome	Croome Court
Croome Park Wall	Ice House, Croome
Croome Farm	Airfield Buildings
Temple Greenhouse	Island Summer House
Boat House Bridges	Owls House
Croome River	Pirton Pool
Knights Hill Pool	Panorama Tower
Worcester Lodge	Pirton Court
Pirton Church	Pirton Court New Farm House
Pirton Court Farm Cottages	New House Farm, Clifton
Sandford Villa Farm	Sandford Villa Cottages
Sandford Lodge	Sandford Forge
Sandford Bolt	The White House, Clifton
Westfield Farm	Butchers Farm
Severn Stoke Old School	Severn Bank House
Severn Bank Lodge	Severn Bank Stables
Park Farm	Park Farm Cottages
Hazeldene Farm	Hazeldene Farm Cottages
Ryalls Court Farm	Moat Farm
Manor Farm, Hill Croome	Manor Farm Cottages
Earls Croome Court	Earls Croome Court Lodge
Earls Croome Vicarage	Earls Croome Church
Earls Croome Cottages	Dunstall Farm
Dunstall Farm Cottages	Dunstall Castle
Red Deer Farm	Millpond Farm
Racing Stables, Kinnersley	Oak Farm, Kinnersley

Nurse Robs, Kinnersley

All Cottages, Kinnersley

Kinnersley Farm

Kinnersley Court Farm

Sewerage Beds, Defford Airfield

Flood Gates, River Severn

Hollybeds Farm (private)

Tirley Court Farm

Deerhurst Priory Farm

Crane Hill Farm

Woolstone Farm

Woolstone Church

Manor Farm, Powick

Manor Farm Cottages

Woodmans Cottage

Lordswood Cottage

Stockend Farm

Stockend Farm Cottages

Ridgeway Farm

Sandpits Farm

Woodmancote Farm

Punch Bowl Gates, Croome

Dry Arch, Croome

Hospital Site Buildings, Croome

Hollygreen Farm

Hemmingfield Cottage

Sheepcote Farm

High House Farm

Levant Lodge

Levant Lodge Stables

Levant Lodge Cottage

Coach House, Levant

Day House Cottages

The Old Boat House, Croome

The Grotto, Croome

Main Drive, Croome

Round House, Baughton Hill

Croome Hunt Kennels

Croome Hunt Cottages

Croome Hunt – Huntsmans House

Perrywood Main Drive

Townstreet Farm, Tirley

Kerswell Green Farm

Borders Farm, Defford.

Vehicles which have been at the Estate since I first worked in 1953:

Agent – Col. Osbert Smith

Very large car

Agent – Mr Chesterman

Austin 16 black

Sub agent – Mr Eastment

Ford Popular blue

Clerk – Mr Hartland

Standard 10 black

Foreman – Dai Partridge

Ford Popular Van grey

Forester – Mr Faithfull

Square Ford black

Estate Lorry Forestry Dept.

Ford grey

Clerk of Works – Ken Sheppard	Ford Popular Van grey
Clerk of Works – Tom Keith	Austin A35 blue
Clerk of Works – George Kingdon	Austin A35 blue
Agent – D Meyrick	Consul
Foreman – Bill Talbot	Bedford Dormobile brown
General use – Building Dept.	Bedford blue
Estate lorry – B Overton	Austin
General Building Dept.	Austin pick-up blue/brown
General Building Dept.	Bedford
General Forestry Dept.	Bedford
General Forestry Dept.	Land Rover long wheel base
General Forestry Dept.	Land Rover short wheel base blue
Estate lorry Building Dept.	Bedford brown
Agent – J Henderson	Marina brown

Farmers I have known:

Mr Page / Mr Stone	High Green Farm
Mr Scott / Mr Troughton / Mr Wiggan	Croome Farm
Mr Chipp	Sermans Farm, Pirton
Mr Clift	Church Farm, Pirton
Mr B Kitchener	Elm Farm, Pirton
Mr G Corbett	Swanbrook Farm, Pirton
Mr P Baxter / Mr Jenkins / Mr Hurst	Pirton Court Farm
Mr C Nixon	Kinnersley Court Farm
Mr Chandler	Kinnersley Farm
Mr L Rimell	High House Farm
Mr D Rimell	Dunstall Farm
Mr P Rimell	Kerswell Green Farm
Mr B Collin	Butchers Farm/Westfield Farm
Mr T Page / Mr Lole	Hermitage Farm
Mr Watkins	Sheepcote Farm

Mr N Revill	Sandford Villa Farm
Miss Stokes	Naunton Farm
Mr T Nixon	Naunton Smallholding
Mr J Gittins / Mr C Gittins	Clifton Court Farm
Mr Latham / Mr C Gittins	Lower Farm, Clifton
Mr Spiers	Hollygreen Farm
Mr D Spiers / Mr A Spiers	Manor Farm, Hill Croome
Mr Chugg / Mr Herbert	Red Deer Farm
Mr Allard	Woodmancote Farm
Mr Evans	Church Farm, Grafton
Mr L Page	Libbery Farm
Mr Bakewell	Yew Tree Farm, Libbery
Mr Rolls	Court Farm, Upton Snodsbury
Mr Tarran	Holy Oak Farm
Mr T Bomford / Mr J Bomford	Allesborough Farm
Mr C Hodgetts	Park Farm, Kempsey
Mr Floyd	Stock End Farm
Mr Tooby / Mr Hawkins	Manor Farm, Powick
Mr M Rankin	Ridgeway Farm, Powick
Mr Watkins	Sandpits Farm, Powick
Mr ?	Woolstone Hill Farm
Mr Daniels	Crane Hill Farm
Mr G Bayliss	Hurst Farm, Wyre
Mr F Rimell	Racing Stables, Kinnersley
Mr H Smith	Narrow Wood Farm, Wadborough
Mr L Hampton	Pirton House Farm
Mr A Radburn	Firs Farm, Drakes Broughton
Mr T Lewis	Walcott Farm, Drakes Broughton
Mr T Jones	Lower Walcott Farm
Mr J Morris	Caddicroft Farm
Mr Jones	Chevington Farm

Mr G Surman / Mr P Surman	Ryalls Court Farm
Mr I.Jones	Naunton Farm, Stokes Bomford
Mr I Jones / Mr T Nixon	Birch Farm
Mr E Gerrard	Millpond Farm
Mr Checketts	Farm at Drakes Broughton
Mr Perks	Pinvin Smallholding
Mr C Harber	Baughton Hill Farm

Listed below are materials and plant which was stored at the hospital building once they had been prepared by myself and the lorry driver for the Estate, Brian Overton. The rough carpenter made up racking for the various items, all from timber off the Estate.

Cast iron half round guttering and fittings 4", 4.5" and 5"
Cast Iron rainwater downpipes and fittings 2", 2.5" and 3"
Galvanised half round guttering and fittings 3" and 4"
Galvanised rainwater downpipes and fittings 2" and 3"
Asbestos half round guttering and fixings 4", 4.5", 5" and 6"
Asbestos rainwater downpipes and fixings 2", 2.5", 3" and 4.5"
Asbestos soil pipes and fittings 4"
O.G. cast iron guttering and fittings 4" and 4.5"
Galvanised tube ¾", 1", 1 ¼", 1 ½" and 2"
Kee Klamp tube fittings
Galvanised cattle drinking troughs
Tiled surround fireplaces
Rayburn solid fuel cookers
Steel lintels
Concrete lintels
Airbricks
Quarry floor tiles 6 x 6" 8 x 8" and 9 x 9"
Windows wooden
Windows metal
Doors, all sizes

Stable doors
Barn doors
Polythene water tube ½", ¾", 1", 1 ½" and 2"
Nuralite sheeting 8'x 3'
Balloon guards for soil pipes
Various cast iron baths
Basins and toilet pans
Belfast sinks
Newtonite lath
Electrical fittings
Asbestos roof sheeting – Standard, Big 6, Trafford tile
Smoke pipe vitreous enamel 4" and 5"
Smoke pipe asbestos 6"
Elson toilets
Galvanised fly mesh for larder windows
Clear Perspex sheeting, standard corrugation
Gates wooden
Gates galvanised
Cattle yard farm gates
Large window frames
Fire bricks, baskets and frets
Galvanised bull pen gates
Angle iron
Staddle stones
Breeze blocks
Plasterboard
Baseboard
Slate roofing
Stone copings
Rock faced concrete blocks
Curved asbestos roof sheets
Filon sheeting
Blue stone pavers
Local stone
Glazed stoneware drain pipes 1st grade 4" and 6"

Glazed stoneware drain pipes 2nd grade 4", 6" and 9"
Glazed stoneware drain pipe fittings 4", 6" and 9"
Glazed stoneware drain gullies, P, Q and S traps
Clear perspex sheeting big 6 profile
Concrete building blocks 4", 6" and 9"
Agricultural drain pipes 3", 4" and 6"
Bricks new, all makes
Bricks second hand
Chimney pots
Chimney cowls
Large floor stones
Drain gratings
Roofing tiles
Pantiles
Ridge, valley and hip tiles
Lead sheeting
Steel roof trusses
Tile battening
1000 gauge polythene film sheeting
Glass roof tiles
Cement – ordinary and masonry
Lime
Thistle plaster
Large salvaged barn timbers
Building sand
Concrete mix ¾" gravel/sand
Granite dust
Various hardware
Top soil

The storage of building materials and plant were stored as follows
(list to be read with attached plan):
Room No.

1. Asbestos H.R. Guttering and asbestos R.W. Downpipes and
   fittings

2. Firebacks, fret baskets and air bricks
3. Tiled fireplace surrounds and Rayburn solid fuel cookers
4/5. Front hall – kept clear
6. Rayburn cooker parts, flue pipes and fittings
7. Firebricks
8. Galvanised H.R. guttering and galvanised rainwater downpipes and fittings
9. Galvanised and concrete lintels
10. Cement, lime, plaster, plasterboard and baseboard
11. Was for concrete block making. New double doors fitted to this room and then turned into builders plant store
12. Cast iron rainwater downpipes and fittings
13. O.G. cast iron guttering and fittings
14. Cast iron H.R. gutter fittings
15. Cast iron H.R. guttering
16. Passage kept clear
17. Lobby kept clear
18. Scrap lead, waiting to be bagged and weighed
19. Scrap copper and brass, waiting to be bagged and weighed
20. This room was used for oiling and servicing scaffold fittings
21/22. Asbestos roof sheeting, various types
23. Galvanised corrugated sheeting and perspex sheeting
24. Second hand chimney pots and cowls
25. Part of this area used to store 21' lengths of galvanised tube
26. Wooden doors and gates
27. Wooden windows
28. Glazed stoneware rainwater gullies, P, Q and S traps and gratings
29. Metal framed windows
30. Alkathene water supply pipes
31. Floor tiles
32. Glazed stoneware drainage bends and channels

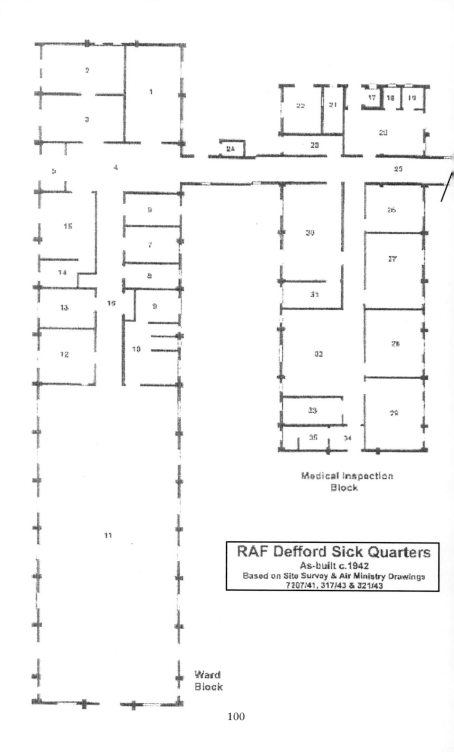

Medical Inspection
Block

RAF Defford Sick Quarters
As-built c.1942
Based on Site Survey & Air Ministry Drawings
7207/41, 317/43 & 321/43

Ward
Block

100

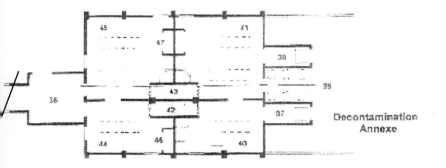

Decontamination Annexe

	Ward Block	
1	Accident & Reception Ward	19ft 8in by 11ft 8in
2	Officers' Bathroom & Toilet	9ft 11in by 16ft 4in
3	Officers' Ward (not original size)	9ft 7in by 16ft 4in
4	Hall	9ft 3in by 22ft 8in
5	Entrance Lobby (blackout porch)	4ft 8in by 9ft 3in
6	Ward Equipment Store	6ft 6in by 11ft 8in
7	Linen Store	7ft 2in by 11ft 1in
8	Sluice	5ft by 11ft 1in
9	Bathroom	6ft 9in by 8ft 5in
10	Toilets & Washroom	12ft 6in by 11ft 1in
11	Airmen's Ward	28ft by 65ft
12	Nursing Duty Room	11ft 8in by 11ft 2in
13	Unknown	8ft by 11ft 2in
14	Bathroom	5ft 7in by 7ft 3in
15	Observation Ward	11ft 2in by 13ft 6in
16	Corridor with two cupboards	5ft by 40ft 6in
	Medical Inspection Block	
17	Lobby & Fuel Store	4ft by 7ft
18	Larder	3ft 6in by 4ft
19	Store	4ft by 4ft
20	Kitchen	9ft by 16ft
21	Fuel Store	4ft by 9ft 6in
22	Boiler Room	7ft 6in by 9ft 6in
23	Dirty Linen Store	4ft by 12ft
24	Fuel Store	3ft by 4ft 6in
25	Main Corridor	5ft by 59ft
26	Office	9ft 8in by 11ft 2in
27	Medical Officer's Consulting Room	11ft 9in by 15ft 8in
28	Dental Surgery	11ft 9in by 13ft 6in
29	Dental Surgery	11ft 9in by 14ft
30	Medical Inspection	11ft 9in by 15ft 9in
31	Dispensary	5ft 6in by 11ft 5in
32	Waiting Room	16ft by 17ft 7in
33	Dental Store	5ft 7in by 11ft 5in
34	Lobby	4ft 10in by 5ft 7in
35	Toilet & Washroom	4ft 10in by 10ft 8in
	Decontamination Annexe	
36	Hall	10ft by 11ft
37	Female Entrance	4ft by 9ft
38	Male Entrance	4ft by 9ft
39	Dirty Clothes Bins	7ft by 9ft
40	Female Undressing & Cleansing Room	10ft 9in by 17ft 3in
41	Male Undressing & Cleansing Room	15ft 6in by 17ft 3in
42	Female Airlock	3ft by 9ft
43	Male Airlock	3ft by 9ft
44	Female Dressing Room	10ft 9in by 17ft 3in
45	Male Dressing Room	15ft 6in by 17ft 3in
46-47	Clean Clothes Store (Bleach Store behind)	11ft 9in by 4ft 6in

33. Electrical goods
34. Lobby kept clear
35. Various broken items
36. Rolls of Newtonite lath
37/38. Demolished
41/47. Some partition walls were removed by Estate staff. This building was then used to store farm equipment i.e. galvanised cattle troughs, drinking bowls and Kee Klamp fitting for cattle yard fencing.

Builders plant (see Room 11 on plan):
Concrete mixers
Motorised concrete tamper
Scaffolding and fittings
Planks of all sizes
Tower scaffold
Chimney scaffold
Steel trestles
Wooden trestles
Acro props
Sack trucks
4 wheel flat trolley
Rota scaffold hoist and attachments
Concrete steel road forms and pegs
Water storage tanks
Builders 6 x 3' sieve
Garden rollers
Wheelbarrows
Cement storage boxes
Concrete block machine manual and electrical
Tarpaulins, all sizes

Builders site huts and material huts
Portable toilets
Builders site boards
Trestles for plasterer's stand
Hose pipes
Large ground roller
Trailing mole plough
Water pump
Hand winch
Steel tripods for road forms
Wire rope and chains

A Change of Direction

Before I went into the office I was on the tractor – a Ferguson tractor with a front loader – and George Kingdon used to ask me to drive this. I also delivered hardcore and other goods from Defford camp where they had all the waste tarmac. I used to enjoy driving the tractor. This went on for about six months in 1961.

One day when I was again working with Fred Gerrard, as his labourer had left, we were in the process of doing the alterations to Croome Farm Cottages which is down a lane opposite Flower Garden Cottage. George Kingdon happened to come to the site, this was September in 1961, and asked Fred if he could spare me for a couple of hours to go out with him on a survey. As there were other men working on the site, Fred wouldn't be working on his own, so off I went with George Kingdon to do some site measurements at Narrow Wood Farm Wadborough where there was a new farm building planned to be put up.

Once we had got everything marked out George asked me if I would set up the siting rods so he could look through the Cowley and take some levels of the waste lands where the building was going to be built. When we had done this, we were there for about two and a half to three hours, and got back to the little A35 van – he remarked that I had read the measurements off as if I had done it before. I said I had worked on Defford camp with a building contractor for some years before I came on the estate and I used to go out with the Clerk of Works of the building firm then and many a day we would go out doing surveys so I knew how to read the site measurements.

After that, every time there was a new building to be put up on the Estate, Mr Kingdon would come to site and ask if Fred could spare me and off we would go again. There were a lot of new buildings going up at that time as many of the old buildings were being pulled down, farming was changing. Atcost and Crendon concrete buildings were being put up and each time there was a survey to do.

It was during one of these visits, in October 1961, to The Hurst in Wyre where we were putting up a new cattle building, when we were putting all the gear back into the van that George Kingdon asked me if I would be interested in working in the office. He wanted a full time storeman. At that time the lorry driver would keep a note of materials being booked in and out, but it needed a full time storeman because there were going to be more men taken on. I said that I really didn't want to work in an office as I'd worked in one on Defford camp and didn't really want to go back into office work again.

The following week we were still out at Croome Farm Cottages doing the alterations and on the Tuesday Mr Kingdon came along again and off we went to a survey at Park Farm, where another big cattle yard building was going up. When we were wrapping everything up, we went back to the van and the question arose again, I was asked if I would take this job on. He had noticed how tidy I was around the sites, how clean and tidy everything was and how I used to look after the concrete mixers and keep everything up together. Again he asked me if I would take this job and again I said no, I didn't really want to do it.

Later, in November I had once again been moved from working with Fred and I was helping Bill Overton down at Ryalls Court

Farm, which was Peter Surman's dad's farm at Upton-upon-Severn. We were busy taking some old buildings down, taking the thatch off a building and George Kingdon called in on the Tuesday and took me to one side and again I was asked about the job. As it was the third time he had asked me and he was really serious about me taking this job, I eventually gave in and said I would take it on. That was on Tuesday, 14 November. For the next two days I still helped Bill Overton because he couldn't manage on his own, but on the Friday of that week, the 17 November, I reported to the office with my shoes blacked, and brown bib'n'brace overalls on. Mr Kingdon had had a brand new desk made for me by Albert Gerrard. This Store Keeper's position was going to change my life completely. It was a big challenge for me and with Mr Kingdon as my boss, it put me in good stead when he left the Estate and the likes of Jenks, Hamer and Pinnock came on the scene with G W Coventry Ltd in 1976.

George Kingdon had his drawing table plus a desk in this office and there was a small cupboard which came out of one of the RAF buildings plus a tall cupboard where all the files were kept, which came from Severn Bank House. My desk was pushed up into the corner. The electrician came and put a light over the desk. We had one double bar electric fire, which we had to share, which was always switched off before Col. Osbert Smith visited the office, which he used to do every morning to find out where the Estate staff were working. Behind Mr Kingdon's desk was a blackboard which had to be written out with chalk every morning stating what jobs were going on and which men were at which site.

The first morning I was shown all the paperwork which had been put in boxes, all the external and internal order books and George Kingdon said "I'll leave you to it." We'd got all new ledger books, and he had also ordered a complete new stock card system as he wanted everything entered onto stock cards. He also gave me a handbook on estate yard work but I didn't really need much showing because I'd been a Stores Controller on Defford camp and with more men than we had on Croome Estate. The priority was to get the stores sorted out. George Kingdon and the driver of the lorry would give up the ordering of materials, and that would be my job.

My duties as Stores Controller were all hand written out by Mr Kingdon. Unfortunately, I have lost all these, but my job was to take full control of the stores, not only at High Green, but also at Croome where the buildings were called the Hospital Site. This name was given to the site because it was an RAF Building on Defford camp during the war time and now was vacant and a lot of the stores for Croome kept were there.

We had our own petrol pump in the yard which took 200 gallons of petrol because not only was there the Clerk of Works' van, plus other Estate vehicles, and the forestry department vehicle, we also had a diesel tank which was filled for the tractors for the forestry and building departments and to order the fuel was also going to be my job. At that time, Mr Hartland was the estate clerk and he came up to the office and we went out and dipped the tank, he gave me the book and the keys and said it was now up to me, and that was my first day at Croome as Stores Keeper. My works contract was altered and my title was no longer labourer, it was changed to Stores Keeper.

The Estate Office in those early times was very busy and Mr Hartland the Estate Clerk used to run it like clockwork. He was very good at figures. No calculators then, nor adding machines, but he could run up a row of figures and get the right total in no time at all – a brilliant man.

When I first entered the office, Mr Hartland was very helpful to me and showed me the ins and outs of figure work. At that time in the office, there was the land agent, Mr Hartland, and a lady secretary. This was a very busy Estate with a building department, forestry department plus two Home Farms. Once I got into the office at 8 am I did not stop working until lunch time. Workmen and delivery lorries would be arriving all the time. To my surprise, I loved the job I was doing.

My first job was to look through all the books, but on a Saturday morning when all the lorries had gone out and all the men had gone to their jobs I would start looking in the stores, taking a note of everything and making notes of how I was going to alter things. We hadn't got the Estate Yard then, not the stores area, all the stores were up at Croome. Mr Kingdon and I had to go up on a Saturday morning and unlock the gate by Fred's and go and have a look round. It was very untidy and I was told by Mr Kingdon that everything had got to be altered and I was to do it my way as I was going to be in charge of everything. He handed me the keys and said "It's all yours Mal". If I wanted any help then I could have Brian Overton, but not in the daytime, it would be at night-time, and we could get a couple or three hours in at night, and we would be paid ordinary rate, not overtime rate. I didn't mind this because I knew there was a big job in hand to do.

Hospital Site Building – Airmen's Ward (now being used as National Trust Canteen) had been part of RAF Defford, and this building was one of the hospitals of the camp. The large double doors were put into this building not long after the Estate took over the site. Firstly, the airmen's ward was used to make concrete building blocks. Once the manufacture of these blocks had stopped, the building was used to store building plant in. My new job was to take over all the stores, not only at High Green, but also at the Hospital site.

The first thing I did was to have a good look round. Some weeks before I had removed all the internal doors to make for easier movement of materials. All the doors which were taken off were measured and the sizes written on them and they were then entered on the stock cards. There were various rooms and it was up to me to decide which room should store which items. We had a rough carpenter on the forestry side, and again with the Agent's permission we got him to make up some rough storage racks from some 4 x 2s which we would put all the cast iron guttering and asbestos on. I had a room for guttering, one for Rayburn cookers – you name it we had it there and were more than likely going to run out of room. All the glazed stoneware drainage materials were stored inside, all the bends and channels and again this was all going to be sorted out but the first thing was to get all the doors off so we could get in and out. Once the inside was sorted out, which took Brian and I nearly six weeks it was then up to me to mark all the rooms which I had sorted with black paint, marked all from A right through and these letters would correspond to my stock cards. Take for instance 'A' which was the first room inside the Hospital Site. This had cast iron guttering, not rainwater pipes, they were in separate rooms, so if I happened to be off sick George Kingdon would look on the 'A' stock card to find if we had the cast iron goods in stock.

This again I did on my own at night because it wasn't a two handed job and again I got it sorted out. The next job Brian and I had to tackle was the outside, because although there were a lot of concrete roads at the Hospital Site a lot of them were overgrown and we had to set about cutting all that undergrowth back. We had to restack all the bricks, pipes, roof tiles etc., so that they were easier to handle and again it was left to me to count all these, and there would be an item on my stock card for heavy building goods, or in my book.

I then made a farm equipment store, still at the Hospital Site. This store was to hold cattle troughs, Kee clamp fittings, thousands of feet of galvanised tube which was used for cutting and then making legs for the cattle troughs and loads more fittings.

Once the Hospital Site Stores was completed my next task was to sort out the Estate Yard at High Green. I tackled the General Store first, it needed new shelving and racking. This was constructed by the Estate rough carpenter, Arthur Turk (his father Alf was the sawyer in the Estate Sawmill), all the tools were shelved and everything had its place. I then knocked out the old wheelwrights fireplace and installed shelving to take all the Rayburn fire bricks, again everything was entered onto stock cards. I then, with the Rayburn bricks put in place, had to count them and by this time Mr Peplow of Sharpe & Fisher had got the Rayburn catalogues for nearly every Rayburn which I asked him for and I soon knew every part, and all these were entered onto the stock cards. In time the Clerk of Works sent me to properties to inspect and order any items which required replacement.

My next job was to organise the plant. As you can imagine, there were ladders, trestles and steps. Every twelve months I had to go round to each site taking an inventory of all the steps and plant which was prepared for Mr Hartland. I priced it and Mr Hartland went through it. There were boxes of old numbers in the stores when I took over and I spent hours at night screwing door numbers to the inside of the ladders and the steps, the painters trestles and everything else that I could, and put in whether it was a thirty rung pole ladder or a twenty four-twenty four extension ladder. They would all have different numbers and these numbers would be put on the stock cards. At the end of the year I would go round the site and check the stock cards. I had started 1961 in the office and this was now nearly twelve months on and I was still sorting out the stores. The stock cards arrived eventually, and Mr Kingdon got Donald Keitley, who was apprentice to Tom Grinter, to make some stock card boxes with partitions in them and they had all got to be lettered under their own headings.

We had no filing cabinets in the office, the estate wouldn't go to the expense of buying them, and there were no drawers in my desk, so all we had were three or four second hand cupboards which came off Defford camp. I had to sort out Mr Kingdon's drawer with all the files in, so I had my work cut out, but it was a challenge I was looking forward to and eventually got stuck into it.

Once all the rooms had been made ready to receive building materials, the stock card system was up and running, and the rooms were marked to correspond with my stock card system. The only time I went to Croome was if there was a delivery or the Estate lorry had to visit to collect materials. I had to go with them to unlock the gate and stores and I would assist with either loading or unloading. Some days I would have a few hours at Croome on my own to just make checks on materials and to sweep through, after I had finished

Malcolm Walford, 1963

you could have eaten off the floor. I was very proud of the Stores and the work Brian Overton and I had carried out, working in the evening at flat rate wages to get the buildings sorted out in order to take the materials which were going to be stored there. Due to improvements being made to cottages and farms, quite a lot of building materials were going to be stored there. I remember those days as if it was yesterday, singing away to myself in those buildings. Some days when I had been at Croome, the only person I saw was Fred Gerrard's wife, Marion collecting her car from the old ambulance garage to go to work.

I used to take stock card boxes home to work on, which wasn't really fair on Mary and the kids. I was missing a lot of the time watching the children growing up because of my involvement with Croome Estate, but I had a job to do and I was either going to do it properly or not at all.

The stock card system was completed after two years and everything was then accounted for. The stores were kept under lock and key and nothing was taken out without my or Mr Kingdon's authority. Mr Kingdon was very strict about this because it had taken some time to set up. If he came over to the stores on a weekend and wanted any item, there was always a note on my desk on Monday with his signature on.

The wheelwright's shop had already been turned into a store when I started at the Estate. When I took over the stores, I found bags and bags of nails and loads of cooking ranges still in their cardboard packaging. Why they had ever been ordered I do not know. I enquired of Mr Kingdon what was to be done with these and he told me it was my job to sort things out. So they all ended up going for scrap, they all had to be weighed at the old weighbridge at Baynhall before being taken to Worcester. The bags of nails had just built up through giving reps orders for nails over the years and they had just been chucked on the floor with the labels still on them. There were some nail boxes – lovely nail boxes – already built in there out of estate timber, but there were no markings on the front of these boxes and this had all got to be altered. I had my own ideas about what I wanted to do and it might take me a long time to do it, but it had got to be done.

I used to stay on at night, even though I didn't get paid for it, and start going through the order books to familiarise myself with the Rayburns etc. on the estate. Because nearly every house on the estate had a Rayburn cooker I wanted to find out the details of these cookers so I could order the parts and get all the details right.

My duties were not only taking on the large stores, but also helping Mr Kingdon with various site works.For instance, the surveys of several Estate farms where new concrete and steel framed buildings were going to be sited, and also what we called Pole Barn buildings made out of second hand telegraph poles and corrugated tin for the roofs and side sheetings. Some of the sites we worked on were:

Narrow Wood Farm	Atcost concrete framed buildings
Park Farm	Crendon concrete framed buildings
Woolstone Hill Farm	Crendon concrete framed buildings
Westfield Farm	Crendon concrete framed buildings
Sheepcote Farm	Crendon concrete framed buildings
Manor Farm, Hill Croome	Dairy and cattle yard buildings
Hermitage Farm	Concrete framed buildings
Clifton Lower Farm	Steel framed buildings
Pirton Court Farm	New grain store
Sermons Farm, Pirton	Concrete framed buildings
Ryalls Court Farm	Concrete framed buildings etc.
Woodmancote Farm	Concrete framed buildings and Pole barn

The Hurst, Wyre	Pole barn
Forestry Yard	Pole barn to cover treatment tank
Croome Farm, Airfield	Concrete framed buildings
Allesboro Farm	Concrete framed buildings

There could be others I have missed. Mr Kingdon had drawn all the plans for these and then provided me with a material list so that I could order building materials a couple of weeks before the workmen were due on site. It was a good system.

In addition to all this, I was still going out with George Kingdon to carry out surveys. We would go off in the morning but always came back for lunch, some times stopping at the yard and other days I went home to Pirton School where then I lived. I mostly stopped at the yard to have a quick dinner and then get on with more work. I also had to do the costing sheets. When George Kingdon could see I knew what I was doing, he asked me to do all the time sheets and all the costing sheets, putting the men's hours on, taking the men's hours off the time sheets and booking them to different jobs.

I also had to start a job number book. Every job on the Estate had a number and that number was put to the time sheet. I made sure everybody brought their time sheet in on a Saturday morning. First thing on a Monday morning, when the men had gone off from the yard and the stores had been used and the lorries loaded, it was my job to get back in the office and sort out the time sheets. I used to sign them and then give them to George Kingdon. He would then countersign them and they were handed to the bottom office for Mr Hartland to calculate the wages which were paid on a Wednesday. They were, when I was first on the Estate, paid every fortnight, but I think that the men had gradually got to the stage when they would like their wages every week, so eventually wages were paid once a week and Mr Hartland used to go down to Lloyds Bank in Upton, collect the cash and make the wages up. He would then give them to Mr Kingdon who would take them round the sites some time on a Wednesday.

If Mr Kingdon was away, then they would be handed to Bill Talbot, the General Foreman. Bill Talbot was also sitting his Clerk of Works exam. Things were not very good between Mr Kingdon and him. When he passed his Clerk of Works exam, it seemed the Estate was being run by two bosses, which didn't work. Eventually Bill Talbot gave his notice in, and moved on to another Estate.

At the south end of Croome River there was a sluice gate and during the winter Mr Kingdon and I would have to visit and put a bar in the sluice bolt and lift it to lower the water level in the river. At this time we used to drive down Westfield Lane and across the fields in the Estate A35 van. The fields were all grassed down and Hereford cattle would be grazing on Westfield Farm which was then managed by the Estate. When Bert Collins took over this farm, although it was still owned by the Estate, the land was all ploughed up right to the edge of the river.

A new relief sluice was put in by the Estate building department and a new sluice board made, with a grille at the top of the board. This was the winter sluice board. A second sluice board was made, a full board, and this was the summer board and kept the river water at a certain height. When we had to change from summer to winter board, because the grounds had been ploughed up, Mr Kingdon and I would drive to Dunstall Farm and carry the winter board through the farmyard and across the fields, and the summer board had to be carried back for safe keeping at the Estate yard. We were always glad to get back to the yard and have a cup of tea!

At the Grotto we had problems when the Caravan Club came to stay in the Court grounds during the time the nuns were there. They let out some ground just inside the Marble Arch at the Court on the area where the Officer's Mess used to be. These caravan people would be everywhere, all over the churchyard at Croome Church where, I'm sorry to say, a lot of small statues on the graves were taken. The children used to climb over the top of the Grotto building and either Mr Kingdon or myself had to tell them it was private land.

Lots of thieving went on at Croome – lead was ripped off the Island Summerhouse, then the lead was stolen off Temple Greenhouse, and shells were taken from the front of Sabrina at the Grotto, never to be found. The lead was also stolen off Worcester Lodge.

During the building of the M5 motorway in the 1960s the old RAF buildings had been rented out by the Estate to a large firm called Monks to keep and repair large vehicles etc. The Iron Bridge at Croome was damaged by one of these contractor's lorries. The Bridge was hit by the crane on the back of the lorry which had not been lowered and the bridge was damaged beyond repair, so it was decided that the bridge be removed and cut up on site. This was done by Estate workers and the metal then went for scrap. The Coventry Coat of Arms which were each side of the bridge, had been painted by the Estate painters on various occasions, and were cut from the metalwork once the bridge was demolished and stored at High Green Yard. They were then built into the new wall at the Estate Yard during the alterations in 1968/9. There was a bottle with various names of estate workers put inside one of the gate piers. I had to get copies of these coats of arms made in fibre glass and they are fitted into the entrance drive walls leading to the late eleventh Earl of Coventry's home, Earls Croome Court, in 1978/80.

At this time, there was a Trustees Meeting every four months. The Trustees then were Col. Osbert Smith, who was the Senior Trustee and lived at Levant Lodge, Earls Croome, and two others Col. Barker and Major Rowcliffe who lived further away and, when attending meetings, stayed overnight at Levant Lodge. They would arrive in their chauffeur driven cars which would be parked up by the joiners' shop. The chauffeurs would get out their polish and clean the cars while the meeting was going on.

All the Estate vehicles were also put on to stock cards and a note of any repairs was made, including any replacement tyres. If the vehicles had to go to Abbey Garage, Pershore to be serviced, this was also noted, not only on stock cards, but when the invoices came in it went into my book.

All the invoices were taken to the bottom office by the postman, none were delivered to our office, then either Mrs Fothergill or Mr Hartland would bring them up to us about ten o'clock in the morning and put them on my desk. They would already have been stamped and I would check them against quotations, make sure the price corresponded to what I had in the file then I would sign them and put them in a tray in George Kingdon's office.He would eventually countersign them, and they would be passed down to the bottom office for payment – no monies changed hands in our office. It was a very, very busy time.

On a recent visit to Croome Court, down in the basement I came across Mr Kingdon's drawing table. He would spend many hours at this table. All the drawings for cottage improvements and new farm buildings were all carried out at it. Late in the afternoons, he would call to me "Mal, I've finished drawing for today, you can clean my instruments". It was my job to wash and dry all the drawing pens etc. and put them back in their boxes ready for another day. He was a hard act to follow. His drawings were very detailed and as I have said before I learned a lot from him and carried on his traditions. Sadly, Mr Kingdon died two years after leaving Croome, what a loss.

When I moved into No. 8 High Green, in 1967, the main office was open from 9am until 5pm and there were four or five people working in the office. During the winter months it was lovely to see the lights on in the offices and workshops. It was quite a sight. The Clerk of Works and myself were always the last to leave. I used to check that all the buildings were locked and the vehicles were in and I always checked the key board to make sure all the keys were in the right place. You never knew when you would be called out at night, so it was essential that the keys were on the right hook. It wasn't very often we had to turn out at night but you knew that there was always the odd time.

Some nights if the Clerk of Works was completing a drawing he would go home, have his tea, then return to his drawing table and some nights I would return to the office if there were some materials lists to go through. Croome Estate was a very busy office but now all has changed. The main office is staffed by two people and the National Trust leases the workshops, yard and our old offices. Still I have good memories of my time at High Green, they were wonderful hard working times.

The village has changed in my time at Croome. There is now no pub, no shop and no Post Office. During the building of the M5 motorway in the sixties, lorries would be queuing up at the shop all day long. When the motorway lorries were using the old RAF buildings at Croome for a servicing area, the lorries would be coming and going all day long. The old Post Office and shop was situated at No. 8 High Green and was run by Mrs Tom Sherwood. Mr Sherwood worked at the Estate building department, therefore it would have been a tied cottage and when Tom passed away, Mrs Sherwood and her daughter moved to Malvern. The shop and Post Office then moved across the road to No. 25 High Green the home of Mr Kingdon, his wife and children.

The Ice House at Croome

This building fell into disrepair and nothing had been done to it for years. The entrance had some rough timber across the doorway to prevent people falling inside. It was decided in the sixties, when the nuns were at Croome Court that because of the small lads at the school, the Ice House should be made safe and filled in. Every scrap of hardcore was found and it was conveyed to Croome by the Estate tractor and trailer and eventually enough rubble was found to fill the Ice House to the top.

Dunstall Castle.

Vandals were always breaking the boarding off the entrance door. It was up to the Estate building department to make it secure (until the next time).

When I was in hospital in 1969 having an operation for a rupture which I suffered unloading some material at the yard, John Henderson kindly brought Mary and my Dad to see me in Worcester. John retired from his job at Croome in 1996. We still see each other at Croome Park or at Severn Stoke Church and talk of old times.

During the 1960s and 70s Mr Kingdon and I used to walk around the grounds of Croome, not only at weekends, but on summer nights. He would sometimes take his little terrier with him. I think I have worked on most of the Estate Farms and Cottages and it was nice to have a variety of work. Never were two jobs the same, always something different. When I took on the office job with Mr Kingdon, and on days when he was busy at his drawing board and some minor works were reported, he would get me to take his A35 van and look at the problem and report back to him. This gave me a good insight to the maintenance works in hand and put me in good stead when I took over the Building Department for eighteen months before His Lordship engaged Jeff Jenks. I have never looked back and have Mr Kingdon to thank for all I learned from him.

I remember the Forestry department nursery at a field just off Madge Hill Lane at the top of Kennel Bank. They were called muniment beds and quite a lot of the local women worked there. The large wooden trays were made in the Estate joiners' workshop. One side of them was covered in sacking to prevent the wind blowing seeds out of the trays. Many of the Estate trees were grown in this nursery and I remember my uncle, Bob Walford, and a couple of forestry workers collecting the seeds off the trees next door to No. 25 High Green. The trees were on the boundary of the Estate Yard.

Boat House Cover

When Sapcotes' were doing a lot of works in the Boat House including works to the Dry Arch, a burnt out vehicle was found near the Grotto with one person inside. I remember that Col. Osbert Smith and Mr David Meyrick were called to the scene by the workmen. The police were called and an incident vehicle was parked at Croome Estate yard. All the villagers, including myself, were questioned. The man's name was Stan Jones and he came from Welland. I was quite shocked when I heard his name because I had known him back in the 1950s when I lived with my parents at Wadborough. He used to run a taxi business and many a time he would take me and my mates to Worcester on a Saturday night. I think my dad, Len, was more shocked than me because he had gone to school with him. My dad was born in 1900 and when the nurse delivered my dad, her next stop was to deliver Stan, so my dad and he were great mates. (They never did find out why the car was burnt out.)

I shall never forget the day the Pickle Yard treatment tank caught

MY LIFE ON THE CROOME ESTATE

fire. The lad who was treating the timber in the tank had got a good fire going and the creosote was boiling, but when dinner time came he went home (he lived in Worcester Lodge). The trouble was, the creosote boiled over, went down the side of the tank and ignited. Mrs Kingdon, the Clerk of Works wife, phoned me at home during lunchtime and said the Forestry Yard was on fire. It was not long before the Upton Fire Brigade arrived, but with so much creosote on fire they had to evacuate the people from their cottages at High Green due to the thick black smoke. They also had to get the police to close High Green village road. The fire did quite a lot of damage, including burning out some trailers. At a later date steel guttering was fitted to the edge of the large creosote tank to prevent this happening again.

At normal times it was great to see the Forestry men preparing timbers, posts, rails etc for treatment in the tanks. They were really good, hardworking men. I remember the ex W.D. lorry bringing large tree trunks to the sawmill ready for the men to cut them up for the building department, and also cutting weatherboards and various other items, a very exciting time. The old tractor had a large winch which once the back grabs had been put into the ground, pulled the large tree trunks out, ready for loading. The saw in the sawmills was at ground level and controlled by levers. It was called a 'Travelling Bench'. When the mill closed down this saw with all the parts numbered was taken apart and transported to new owners in South Africa.

The first thing I did on a Saturday morning, because I was on my own was to fill in the blackboard in the office at the back of the Clerk of Works' desk. This had to be filled in showing where every man was working on a site with all their names. We had a foreman who used to come in to the office on a Saturday morning when the men came in, but Mr Kingdon who normally did not come in on

Saturdays, would perhaps walk across in the morning and ask if everything was alright

There was a hose out on the middle of the yard and one of my jobs was to clean the vehicles, which I didn't mind, although I was to get out of this eventually. I did have a detail of all the jobs I had to do but unfortunately I have lost the paperwork.

On Saturday mornings, after my breakfast, I would take a flask with me and some biscuits. It wasn't very often that Colonel Osbert didn't come up to the office. He would come to the door, knock, come in and say "Good morning Malcolm" and ask me where the men were. He was a very well thought of and respected man on the Estate. He would always doff his cap when he saw my gran as he rode by, or he would stop and get out of his car and ask her how she was. My gran used to sit outside Rose Cottage in her old rocking chair. He also knew uncle Bob, of course, and got on well with him. He was Senior Trustee and was the man who started me when I first went for my job in 1953.

If it was wet and the men couldn't work outside at their jobs then Mr Kingdon said that rather than have them sitting about, if there was any heavy lifting I wanted doing, I could detail them to do it. On the yard we had the carpenter' shop where there were four full time joiners and their apprentices, working at four joiners' benches. I remember the large open fire in the carpenters' shop. Never a day passed by that there was no fire. I well remember Albert Gerrard cooking his breakfast of a piece of pig meat on some bread. Even Mr Kingdon would remark on it because the wonderful smell drifted into our office.

At the back of the carpenters' shop were some very old and dilapidated tin sheds where all the timber was laid upon old sawn trees, that was how timber was stored, and it meant that there was no way you could measure up to find how much timber there was in stock. There was also another old dilapidated building, filled with beading and Scotia mouldings and architraves, and again this building was smothered in brambles, even inside, and you couldn't see what was there nor could you get in to measure anything.

I also remember the forestry men coming back into the yard on a wet day because if it was raining they had to return to the yard and peel poles ready to be put into the creosote treatment tank. It would generally not be long before Alf Turk had popped home to fetch some home made wine, and not long after this their voices would get louder. Mr Kingdon and I in the office would have a laugh at this. The forestry men were some great workers, no chain saws then, everything done with large cross cut saws – very heavy work. The trees from the Estate woods would be cut down and transported to the Estate sawmills where the forester and his men would cut them into sections on the travelling sawbench. Wonderful days, life on Croome was different to anything you could imagine, with everyone working for one Estate.

About this time, I was introduced to the reps of various building merchants. There was Sharpe & Fisher's rep, Mr Peplow, Western Trading's Mr Jenkins, J R Kents from Gloucester, Mr Bathe, the timber merchants, Rea of Worcester, Mr Partridge and then the rep for MAC of Bristol, Wilf Tromans, who was a big friend of mine.

Other old representatives coming from other builders merchants were Mr Whitehead, from W.F. Bailey's who were based at Silver Street in Worcester who was superseded by a man named Tom Jones when Mr Whitehead retired.

Among my other duties was the job of making sure that all the Estate vehicles were serviced and that the tractors and trailers were not short of parts. I also had to take charge of the parish crockery – all had to be listed and put on the stock cards and any breakages were noted and charged to whoever had borrowed the crockery.

Sometimes, if I had a spare five minutes, I was asked to deliver the tables and crockery either to Severn Stoke Village Hall or Earls Croome or Croome Court or to Earls Croome Court for different functions. Other duties I was supposed to do were; glass cutting and cutting mild steel rods into various lengths for concrete lintels which would be made out on the sites. I used to have to wire all these together, measure it and then put it under a heading for a farm, or property or cottage name, put it in the book and cost it.

During the 1960s the Building department got together a darts team and we used to go round the local pubs playing friendlies for charity and we had some great nights. We played the 'Cabbage Cutters' from Stokes Bomford who played from the Boars Head at Severn Stoke, the darts team from the Rose & Crown at Severn Stoke, the apprentice jockeys from the racing stables at Kinnersley who played at the Oak at Kinnersley, a team at the Yorkshire Grey, and a team at the Gay Dog at Baughton. They were some good nights out and there was always food laid on afterwards. Sad to say the wives were all left at home looking after the children! I eventually joined the darts team at the Rose & Crown, Severn Stoke and we used to play in the Upton-upon-Severn League. It was all local pubs including the Cavalier at Strensham. I played for the Rose & Crown for two to three seasons but when G W Coventry Ltd was formed it was on not many nights that I didn't return to the office to keep up with the paperwork, so this restricted my playing at night. I regret that now.

Another job I was lumbered with happened when people were about to move into one of the Estate cottages. I would be asked to go in a couple of days beforehand and perhaps light a fire and air the house out and clean the bathroom, and make sure the windows were clean. Fortunately at this time I was able to drive the A35 or whichever vehicle was available.

About then, the staff in the main office was increased, there was going to be another lady, so there were going to be two women working in the main office – again the job was advertised, and again I was detailed to fetch the candidates from Worcester. Sometimes I was allowed to use Mr David Meyrick's car which was a Wolseley 1500, to make it more comfortable for them.

Also, when David Meyrick lived at Severn Bank House they used to hold a lot of functions there, so two vehicles were detailed to go down to Upton to carry the food for the caterers and this was a job Brian Overton and I were detailed to do. Two of the vans were cleaned, washed inside and out and made spotless before we would go down and ferry them back. We also had a Bedford Dormobile which had seats in and we could carry the catering people in it. If it was late at night, Brian and I would be asked to come back and take the people home, plus all the catering firm's kit. So as you can see there was a variety of jobs that I was asked to do.

Later, there were more staff taken on and more work was becoming available on the Estate such as a lot of buildings being extended and new farm buildings were being built and also I was still going out with Mr Kingdon on surveys. My job was getting busier, I was ordering more materials and the Hospital site was by then sorted out and everything was on stock cards which made my life a little bit easier. Not only were new materials put onto stock cards, if there was demolition going on on farms or cottages, doors were taken off or windows were taken out. I would measure up every item. I had a pot of paint and a brush at the Hospital site and all the sizes on the windows and doors were marked. All the old gate posts were burnt, but all the gate hangings and fixings were salvaged, you name it everything was salvaged for re-use and it all had to go on the stock cards. You can imagine the thousands of stock cards I had, unfortunately I never kept them, but I wish I had now, because it would have been a good record and people could have seen what went on.

If I ordered two tons of cement, the delivery lorry would reverse through the double doors at the Hospital site, and the driver and I would unload the cement. The cement store at this time was in the old toilet area. It was always very peaceful at this site when I used to carry out stock checking at the end of the year. The only person who I saw was George Proverb, the Gamekeeper, who lived nearby. There were no mobile phones at this time so the only way anybody could contact me was by driving up to the site. These buildings were ideal for storing all the necessary materials and plant in and there was quite a few pounds worth in total.

I'm moving along now to 1968 when George Kingdon said to me one morning that we were going to have a new Stores, the Hospital site was going to be done away with and stocks of materials were going to be run down, we were going to be keeping a minimum stock of different things and there was a new stores and yard going to be built at High Green behind the carpenter's shop. The old sawmill which was on the opposite side of the road from the Estate Office used to employ two men, the sawyer and his lad and they would be cutting up trees all day but eventually the saw mill was closed. During the running of the saw mill and the forestry I used to order a lot of timber off the Forestry department all the sawn timber, whether 3 x 2 or 2 x 2, 6 x 3 which we used to use a lot of, so for anything wanted I had to write an order out for the forester who was in the next office to me and he would put it through and eventually get the timber. But the saw mill was now empty and that was going to be our new timber and plant store. The old building was going to be taken down and the garages were going to be demolished because there were new garages being built on our yard and so there was a big general tidy up. So the next job George

Kingdon and I did was a survey of the back yard which was full of old dilapidated buildings. We were going to take over part of a field which used to be owned by the Estate but was run from the Coventry Arms pub, which used to be a smallholding. We carried out all the surveys and the saw mill timber was done away with and sold. Fred Gerrard and his gang moved into the saw mill they marked all the sheets. New roads were made round the back of the carpenters' shop, and all the ground was dug up. The sawmill was taken down and notices were put on the road at High Green to warn people to 'beware of tractors crossing', because a lot of the soil from off the back of the yard, which was originally the field, was taken and levelled out at the saw mill site. George Kingdon and I measured everything up and the post holes were dug and the saw mill was re-erected behind the carpenters shop. Then we had another farm building erected. This was going to be the new gutter and pipe store, used also for storing doors, and yet another building was erected which was going to be an open fronted garage and then four small garages were built for cars and vans. This all started in 1969.

Eventually, all this work was completed, the saw mill building which was the timber building was painted together with the gutter and pipe store. The tractor and new lorry store couldn't be painted because it had an asbestos roof but all the storage sheds were done, the roads were put in, and the drainage was done, so we were all ready to start. New gravel and sand storage bins were also built with concrete bases.

Both blacksmiths had by now retired and the shop had been altered into a Mess Room for the men, with an electric cooker and everything else, even a drying room.

Going back to the hospital site stores, once it was decided – there was Phase One and Phase Two of the Estate yard being altered, it was my job to organise the men and the transport and start moving stuff down onto the estate yard. There were such a lot of odds and ends at the hospital site that Mr Meyrick, the agent, decided that we were going to have a sale and I was to spend some time with the man from Herbert Banks of Worcester to sort out what was to be sold. There were governess carts and you name it, everything was there, block makers, concrete mixers, troughs, doors, everything, all the old imperial copper fittings were going to be sold. The sale was held and fetched a lot of money, I presume, for the Estate. Soon after this happened, Mr Meyrick unfortunately left and the Trustees then made John Henderson their agent, and he was agent during Phases 1, 2, 3 and 4 of the estate yard alterations. Now the estate yard alterations were not completed until August 1970. Once things were completed and the stores were up and running I had notification that I was to go into hospital to have my rupture attended to. As I suffered with asthma they had to be very careful when I was under the anaesthetic and the operation was carried out at Ronkswood. I did have a rough time. During this time George Kingdon took over the store keeping duties and kept my books up, which was good. The stock cards were all kept up as well. When I came out of hospital I went to see Dr Marshall Wilson, who said I was to have sixteen weeks on the sick, but I could not do that, I wanted to get back to work. So I went over to see George Kingdon and said I wanted to come back to work, then I went to see Mr Henderson, the agent, and he said as long as I had a doctors' note to say I could do light duties, then I could come back. Anyway I went to see the doctor and I got a note to say I could go back to work, but only clerical work, so after about a month I was back at work.

During this time when I went back to work, I had a note from John Henderson saying that as I was not one hundred per cent fit, the Trustees were going to dock my wages, which did not go down very well with George Kingdon because I had gone back early and

MAINTENANCE DEPOT

CROOME   **NEAR WORCESTER**

Situate about 2½ miles from the main Worcester to Tewkesbury
Road (A.38) turning off at Severn Stoke on the road to Pershore.

Dispersal Sale of

SURPLUS BUILDING MATERIALS

AND GENERAL MAINTENANCE EQUIPMENT

also

LANDSCAPE GARDENING MATERIALS

and

Two Concrete Block Making Machines

in all

APPROX. 400 LOTS

all of which

G.   H E R B E R T   B A N K S

have received instructions from The Croome Estate Trust
to sell BY AUCTION UPON THE ABOVE PREMISES

ON SATURDAY 6th FEBRUARY 1971

Sale Commencing at 11 a.m. prompt
Light Refreshments Available.
Mobile Crane Available on the Day of Sale Only.
Auctioneers Offices:
Worcester Street, Kidderminster. Tel: 61981.

MALCOLM WALFORD

BUILDING MATERIALS AND GENERAL PROPERTY
MAINTENANCE EQUIPMENT

viz: Multi-Bloc Minor Concrete Block Making Machine with .95 H.P. Single Phase Electric Motor complete with scraper, moulds, barrow etc., Liner Hand Block Making Machine complete. Two Parker Concrete Mixers with Lister Petrol Engines, Pegson Water Pump with Lister 1. h.p. Petrol Engine, Heavy Hand Winch with brake, Chain Saw, Barford Atom Rotosythe, Tomkin-Darby Trailing Mole Plough, Oxycetelyn Torches, Gauges etc. Ex W.D. Heavy Duty Hand Winch, Chimney Scaffolding Set, Two Sets of Blacksmiths Bellows, Blacksmiths Forge, Anvil, Blacksmiths Tools, Two Lister Water Pumps, Mild Steel Bars, Channel Iron. Angle Iron, Two ¼ h.p. Single Phase Electric Motors, Reinforced Delivery Hose, Hand Tools, Pulleys, Large Quantity Ridges, Tiles, Hips, Valleys, etc. Concrete Roofing Tiles, Flooring Tiles, Roofing Slates, Flooring Tiles, Stone Copings, Concrete Lintels, Rock Faced Concrete Blocks and Facing Bricks, Qty. Glazed Drain Pipes, Breeze Blocks, Big Six Asbestos Roofing Sheets, C.I. Sheets, Roofing Slates, Approx. Seven Hundred Jacksons Wire Cut Bricks, Seven Heavy Elm 17ft. beams, Six Galvanised Water Storage Tanks, Large Quantity Metal and Wooden Window Frames, Two Pairs Stable Type Doors, Four 6ft. Galvanised Cattle Drinking Troughs (new). Metal Garden Gates, Sundry Heavy Duty Pulleys, Large Quantity 1½in. and 1¼in. Kee Clamps, Bull Pen Gate, Ten Pairs of Heavy Wooden Doors, Five Wooden and Glazed Screen Partitions 8ft.6in. x 3ft., Cast Iron 4 inch Piping, Sundry Joinery and General Timber, Glazed Belfast Sinks, Large Window Frame with leaded lights 6ft.9in. x 6ft.9in., Large Quantity Asbestos Down Pipes, Hopper Heads, Bends, Spouting, Angles etc. Approx. 600ft. ½in. and 1in. Galvanised Piping, Curved Asbestos Sheets, Large Quantity of Alkathene Piping ½in., ¾in., 1in. and 1½in., Six Galvanised Water Storage Tanks, 4 sets Roller Conveyors, 10ft. Pair of Heavy Wooden Gates, Large Quantity Electric Light Fittings, Switch and Fuse Boxes etc. Copper Tubing, Cast Iron Baths, Hot Water Tanks, Fire Bricks, Backs and Surrounds, Asbestos Flue Pipes, Cowls etc., etc., Stove Pipe Fittings, Large Quantity Rainwater Pipe Fittings, Guttering etc., Large Quantity Copper Pipe Fittings, Junctions, Bends, Connections, Plumbers Brassware and Copperware, Large Quantity Wood Screws, Coach Bolts, Plumbing Fittings, Rivetts, Bolts etc. Approx. Twenty Tons of Scrap Iron, Copper etc., etc.

LANDSCAPE GARDENING MATERIALS ETC.

viz: Qty. Rock Faced Concrete Bricks, Heavy Slate Trough, 4ft. x 2ft. Twelve Hewn Stone Troughs in various shapes and sizes, Two Hewn Stone Troughs 5ft. x 3ft. x 2ft. Approx. Ten Tons Local Stone, Qty. Blue Stone Paving, Semi-Circular Hewn Stone Trough 4ft. x 2ft. Nine Staddle Stones, Two Cast Iron Water Pumps, Five Spoked Wagon Wheels, Two Cricket Pitch Rolls, Governess Cart, Mill Stone Wheel, Horse Plough.

ALSO

20 ANGLE IRON ROOF TRUSSES 28ft. SPAN

was doing the bookwork plus any other odd jobs which came up whilst also going out surveying with him, although I could not lift anything. Anyway, George Kingdon got me to ring up the Social Services at Worcester, and I had to borrow the van and go in to see the people at Worcester who gave me a book to cover me for my loss of earnings from the Estate. I was not very happy about losing the money, not with the service I was giving the Estate, and nor were my parents. Anyway that was 1969/70 and things eventually got back to normal and I got back doing my proper job.

During the Foot and Mouth outbreak in 1964 bowls of Jeyes Fluid was put outside the offices and workshops for people to clean their gumboots in. The vehicles were kept away from the farms in garages at the rear of the offices. They too were washed down with Jeyes Fluid. What a terrible time that was.

During Christmas periods we would have local carol singers coming round the villages and singing in aid of the Church. Many a time they have sung to me outside my office window. I have spent a lot of time on my own in the office at night. How I regret all that wasted time away from Mary and the children, and I wish I could turn the clocks back. One job I had to do at Christmas time was to ask the Estate building department workmen what size Christmas tree they would like. (All staff were allowed a Christmas tree.) Once I had got all the information and found out how many trees were required, I then gave the order to the Estate forester, Mr Fred Garrard, and the trees were then dug out of the Estate woods and brought to the Estate yard. I would then label them and they would be taken by the workmen just before the Christmas break. Also at this time, the builders merchants' reps would start bringing in gifts to the Clerk of Works office, it could be wine, chocolates, cigarettes, or apples off the market gardening land, or sprouts – quite a mixture. All these items were then put in a cupboard and eventually taken to

CROOME ESTATE TRUST.

Particulars of Terms of Employment given Pursuant to the
Contracts of Employment Act,1963. S.4.

Dated.. 31st January......19 69.

To .Mr. M.Walford.................

From: The Croome Estate Trustees,
        Croome Estate Office,
        High Green,
        Severn Stoke, Worcester.

Your employment in the capacity of. Storekeeper...............
commenced on.. 24th. August.............1953.

The following particulars of the terms of your employment applied
on.....16th. December.................1968.

1. WAGE

(a)   Your wage is £.15...10s...2d.. for a 42¼ hour week. Your wage will be
payable weekly on Thursday made up to the previous Saturday together with a
rent and rate free cottage which you are required to occupy by reason of this
employment.   You are required to keep the interior of the cottage in clean
condition and the garden tidy.

(b)   Your overtime wage for Saturday morning working, when work is available
and weather conditions permit, is £2...15s..8d... provided a full 42¼ hour
week has been worked.

(c)   During the Winter Working period:-

(i) Your wage is £.14,...4s...4d... for a 40 hour week.

(ii) Your overtime wages for Saturday morning working, when work is
available and weather conditions permit, is £.2:...9s:..6d,....
provided a full 40 hour week has been worked.

2. HOURS OF WORK.

(a)   Your hours of work are 7.30.a.m. to 5.0.p.m, Monday to Friday, in
each week. You are entitled to the following meal breaks:- 20 minutes from
9.30.a.m. to 9.50 a.m. and 40 minutes from 1.p.m. to 1.40.p.m.

(b)   Your hours when working on Saturday morning are 7.30.a.m. to 12.20.p.m.
with a meal break of 20 minutes from 9.30.a.m. to 9.50.a.m.

(c)   During the Winter Working period:-

(i) Your hours of work are 8.30.a.m. to 5.0.p.m.,Monday to Friday
inclusive. You are entitled to a meal break of 30 minutes from
12.30.p.m. to 1.0.p.m.

(ii) Your hours when working on Saturday are 8.30.a.m. to 12.30.p.m.

3. HOLIDAYS

You are entitled to two weeks annual holiday each calendar year ending
31st October plus six Public Holidays (namely Good Friday, Easter Monday, Spring Bank
Holiday, Summer Bank Holiday, Christmas Day and Boxing Day) with pay. One week
of the annual holiday to be taken when the Maintenance Department closes down
in the fourth week of August. The remaining week to be taken as a complete week
at any time subject to prior notice from you and agreement with the Employers

- 1 -

4. SICKNESS OR INJURY.

If you are absent from work due to sickness or injury you must send a certificate of incapacity signed by a Doctor within three days to the Estate Office. Further certificates must be sent every week while you remain absent.

You are entitled to sick pay during any period of absence from work due to sickness or injury (for which a Doctor's certificate has been sent when appropriate) not exceeding four weeks in any one calendar year ending 31st October. The amount of any National Insurance benefits received by you will be deducted from your sick pay and you must state how much benefit you receive.

Any payment to you beyond the four week period aforementioned and any payment to you when not entitled to National Insurance benefit will be at the discretion of the Trustees.

5. PENSION

You do participate in the National Graduated Pension Scheme. (No contribution is made to the National Insurance Graduated Pension Scheme in weeks when your earnings do not exceed £9. or an equivalent sum if you are paid at longer intervals or if you are under 18 years of age or over 70 (65 for women).

~~You are not entitled to any other pension by reason of this employment but any payment or allowance which may be made to you will be at the discretion of the Trustees.~~

You are a member of the Estate Retirement Benefit Scheme, details of which are contained in the Rules, a copy of which you have been given.

~~On the 1st July, 19   you will become a member of the Estate Retirement Benefit Scheme if still in this employment and provided you have satisfied the necessary medical requirements of the Scheme. Details of the Scheme are contained in the Rules, a copy of which you will be given when you become a member.~~

Any alterations to the Rules in the Retirement Benefit Scheme will be notified to you in writing.

6. NOTICE.

You must give at least One week's prior notice in writing to terminate your employment to expire on any Friday night.

You are entitled to receive in writing at least.. four.......week's notice to terminate your employment. ~~The period of notice after the dates mentioned will be as follows:-~~

~~After   19   at least   weeks.~~
~~After   19   at least   weeks.~~

Notice of termination of employment by either Party will include the giving up of vacant possession of the cottage referred to above after four weeks from the date of giving the notice.

Received a statement of which the foregoing is a copy

Dated...........................19.......

the agent's office for distribution amongst the office staff.

As you approach the Dry Arch Bridge from the Punch Bowl Gates and carry on over the bridge, you come upon a large heavy white gate, leading to the drive beside the Croome river. The gate was hung on 9" x 9" oak posts and the shutting post was also 9" x 9". These posts were also painted white. The gate used to swing both ways for hunting purposes, and would, I think, have been made by the then Estate joiners. The timbers of the gate were very stout and it also had metal cross members. This gate was there when I started work on the Estate. I presume it was removed by the National Trust when the present gate was fitted.

As I have said, I had worked on most properties on the Croome Estate before I went into the Clerk of Works' Office. Life and works were hard but the work people were wonderful. I had had happy days and sad days. When any of the old workmen passed away the rest of the men always attended their funeral, but that was how close the estate people were, like a large family. In the winter, people who had retired from the estate were always visited and if need be chopping wood and logs were provided.

George Kingdon and Mr David Meyrick were both people you could look up to and so too was Col. Osbert Smith, the Senior Trustee of the Croome Estate. I felt a great deal of responsibility had been put on my shoulders. I was made aware of what was happening on the estate and in some ways I felt I had been put in this position to look after the Coventry estate as best I could. It certainly changed my whole life regarding working for the estate.

Temple Greenhouse

During the 1970s there were again a lot of lead thefts on the Estate. The greenhouse was the first to be attacked with all the lead being stripped off. Instead of lead being put back on the roof areas it was decided to use a new material, Nuralite, which had just come onto the market. The works were carried out and the roof made watertight. At a later date I think lead was once again used on this building.

Island Summerhouse

This building was also targeted by lead thieves when all the ridge capping was stripped off including the lead under the flashings Instead of putting lead back on the ridges it was decided to use blue ridge tiles. These materials were in store at the Estate yard.

Worcester Lodge was also a target for lead thieves in the 1970s. Here again new blue wall cappings were used instead of lead. The Lodge was at that time owned by the Croome Estate Trustees.

Punchbowl Gates

To prevent boy racers driving through the entrance to the Dry Arch, which was a regular occurence, a 4"x 4" oak post was set in concrete in the middle of the entrance. This did not prevent one car becoming wedged on top of the post. It was then decided to make up a special metal barrier, which was made by Swinbourne Bros. of Baughton and fitted by Croome Estate Builders in the 1980s.

After my father Len Walford retired from Railway Service, he took on a job as gardener at Croome Court – during the nun's time there. His job was to keep the shrubbery tidy and any other duties required by the nuns. My wife Mary was also employed at Croome Court during the nun's time, in the sewing room, repairing the boys' clothes, along with other women from High Green village. They would walk to work down Westfield Lane, through Boat House Cover to the Court. Some of the names I remember from that time are; Mabel Compton, Mrs Earle, Mrs Heath, Mrs Cook, Mrs

Garrard, Mrs Jones and Mrs Tustin. Mrs Earle was the mother-in-law of George Kingdon.

We had a very hot summer in the 1970s, the water in the Boat House and Croome River was rapidly disappearing and many of the fish were dying. The Clerk of Works decided that we should take our three inch, Simplite Water Pump down and try to get some oxygen into the water to help the fish. We set it up near the Island Temple and started moving the water around. Mr Kingdon and I worked late into the night after normal work hours and although many of the fish were lost, we did our best. We were very pleased when the weather changed, rain began to fall and the Boat House and River were replenished.

A new bridge was manufactured by J F Hall of Worcester and was put over Croome River to link the Dry Arch to the other side of Boat House Cover. Near the Grotto there were steps formed so that people could walk down to the Sabrina Statue, near the Dry Arch by the pegged fencing, there were also steps made heading down to the bridge. New gravel was ordered to lay on the drive from the Punchbowl Gates up to the Dry Arch.

All this area was going to be opened up to the public one day a week. My job in the Clerk of Works office was to put together a mock-up sign board ready for the proper one to be sign written with prices on. The next thing was to get a collecting box manufactured by Swinbourne Brothers at Baughton, the box welded to a steel post and concreted into the ground. I'm sorry to say this did not stay by the Punchbowl Gates very long before it was ripped from the ground. At this time, Sapcotes' were carrying out a lot of work to replace the stone balustrade to the Dry Arch. I think the new one was constructed in wood. Some stonework to the Island Temple (Summerhouse) was replaced by a firm in Worcester by the name of Ben Davis.

George Kingdon was a very keen fisherman and a member of the Isaac Newton Club. He suggested that several places not only in Boat House Cover, but also down the River should be cleared of reeds and fishing spots should be set up for local people to fish. This was agreed and on various nights several men would visit the river and clear rubbish and set up fishing bays. Quite a few second-hand doors from the Estate yard were used and eventually fishing was carried out. Many a day George Kingdon would say to me "I'm off fishing up the Teme. You know where the men are working on the Estate so there should be no problems" I think he must have had confidence in me and knew if there was a problem I could deal with it.

In the 1970s, the Clerk of Works office was altered, a new doorway was knocked through into the old plumbing store next door and this was altered to form the new office. I was to have an office of my own. Two desks and chairs were purchased, one for the Clerk of Works and one for me. A new hatch was formed where the phone sat and my job was to answer the phone and take calls for the Clerk of Works. I also had to answer the main phone first thing in the morning before the main office opened. Mr Kingdon and I worked very closely together and he showed me how to do various things – this I would appreciate in the following years when he left to join another estate and I was to take over the day to day running of the Estate building department.

At Christmas time, Mary, my late wife, would always bake sausage rolls before the workmen broke up for their Christmas break. I would get the men together in the joiners' shop, get a good fire going and then fetch the food. A good time was had by all and it started Christmas well.

In 1974 I went into the office one morning and George Kingdon dropped a bombshell in saying that he was leaving. After quite a few

Malcolm Walford, 1970s

years with George in the office, I did not know what to expect, but he was taking a Clerk of Works job down in Steyning in West Sussex. He asked if I would go with him but unfortunately my parents were now getting into their eighties and as I was the only son, I did not want to be away down there. I did go down and have a look at the house he was moving into, there was a cottage for me if I wanted it, but I declined the offer. Anyway George was given a presentation by John Henderson and then he left.

I was then left to run the building department on my own. I used to deal with all the paperwork which George had done and I carried on doing that for nearly eighteen months, running all the jobs. One day I was sat in the office and John Henderson brought in a smartish bloke wearing a suit and carrying a brief case. He introduced him as the new Clerk of Works. His name was Jeff Jenks. I was asked to show him all the properties on the estate that we were working on, and show him how things were run in the office and we went from there. After several weeks and my going around several sites where the old workforce were still carrying out maintenance and showing Jeff the works that were being carried out, I thought to myself that I didn't like the ideas that Jeff had and what was about to happen. Still I had a job to do and a job I enjoyed. I had always kept notes of everything which was being done on the Estate and of what was going through the stores, and it was more particular then that I did keep these notes, because they were going to be beneficial to me at a later date.

I was told that the stock card system I had worked so hard on was not to be used in the future (although I did try to keep it going), but with the new directors, the yard and stores were open at all times. As you can imagine, on a Monday morning when I came back into work and went to the stores, I would find there were items missing and not accounted for. It was very disheartening after the system which Mr Kingdon and I had got going.

The main change to the Estate was when the eleventh Earl of Coventry made the Building Department into a company – this company was called G W Coventry Ltd. It started in 1976 and lasted until 1986. The forestry department was closed by the new owners, The Sun Alliance Group. It was very sad to see all the changes and I was very glad that a lot of the old workforce had either retired or passed on. Croome would never be the same again. Jeff Jenks was made Managing Director of G W Coventry Ltd, and a Kerry Hamer and his wife Teresa were both made Directors. It came as quite a shock to me when his Lordship called me to Earls Croome Court and asked if I would be the new Company Secretary. Of course my wages were going to be increased and yes, I accepted the new position. Christine Morgan, who had worked with Lord Coventry at Heenan & Froudes in Worcester, came as secretary to Mr Jenks. Kerry Hamer had bought, or was given, a house called Severn Bank House, by Lord Coventry and various works were being undertaken by his own men to put in an indoor swimming pool. I received a phone call from him one morning stating that high winds had made a large chimney unsafe and could I arrange for some Estate workmen to get to the site as soon as possible. I moved Fred Gerrard and three other men onto the site, and insisted on an inspection. Kerry Hamer was using gipsy labour. They had knocked some central, load bearing, walls out without propping and the roof had started sagging. After several days and lots of Acro props being put in, the men prevented the whole of the roof from collapsing. I had to tell Lord Coventry what had happened and he was not happy. Not long after this a memo came from Lord Coventry stating that no work should be carried out on directors' houses. Mr Hamer was not a happy man, and he still got an invoice for the work.

We were making alterations to Stone Cottage, Croome, near the London Arch, with a view to putting the house up for sale. Mr Hamer had central heating oil delivered to Severn Bank House but someone altered the ticket to read Stone Cottage. I knew this was not true because I had not ordered an oil tank for the cottage and the plumbing work had not even started. Again, an invoice was sent to Mr Hamer.

When I worked for G W Coventry Ltd, we were allowed to go outside the Estate for work and a lot of work outside was undertaken, whereas before, when it was Croome Estate Building Dept., no work was done outside the Estate. So now we started doing work all over the place, even up in Birmingham because Lord Coventry had

Insurance Offices in Birmingham and some of the men were working up there, so it was quite a change and things were not being done by Mr Jenks as George Kingdon would have done them. It was done haphazardly and I did not agree with the way things were working and could not see that this firm was going to go on for a very long time. Anyway, I was told by Jeff Jenks one day that if the firm did not make any money then the building staff would revert back to the Estate. The Estate workers kept their service record during the changeover. The names of the workers were: Fred Gerrard, Albert Gerrard, Sid Collins, Reg Child, Ron Woodyatt, Bill Hooper, Billy Wellon and Brian Overton.

Once I was made Company Secretary of His Lordship's Building Company in 1976 I had more to do with him. I think His Lordship was a lonely man. What hit him hard was losing his son, Viscount Deerhurst. Losing a son, as I have found out, certainly knocks you about.

I had never done VAT or bookwork before, at least, not to the point I was going to have to now. Lord Coventry said that Mr Jenks had somebody in Cheltenham who would come up once a week and show me how to do the books, including the VAT returns, so I was quite happy with that. I had by then got my own car, which I was allowed petrol money for getting around the estate, if Jeff was not there. Anyway I did get on with the VAT books. A man called Tom Roberts came up from Cheltenham, if Jeff did not fetch him then I had to go and fetch him and take him back. There was also another firm started up from the Estate offices, called Arnlaw Developments. This was a firm that Lord Coventry bought out down at Corse Lawn near Tewkesbury, and there was a site there for eight houses, which Jeff Jenks was going to take charge of. Lord Coventry would visit the office regularly and talk to Jeff but always call in and see me in my office.

The first thing Jeff Jenks said was that the office furniture was not good enough and he required a large oval desk. Not long after this I was moved into the old Foresters office and Fred Garrard then used his house as his office. Fred lived at No. 6 High Green, right next to the forestry yard.

New drawings were prepared and the office I was in was going to be demolished. If you look at the old drawings I did some years ago, there was a ten feet wide gap between the old forester's office and my old original office. This was to get the coke trailer through to the storage bins for the old boiler, which kept the main Estate office warm. This gap was going to be infilled leaving a small corridor leading to the main office door. A new hatch was going to be installed in the secretary's office for when people arrived, with new windows, new floors, shelving fitted and of course, an oval desk. This office was going to be used by the MD Jeff Jenks. I was going to be moved into the old Clerk of Works office. These offices still exist today and are used by the National Trust.

The works started at a rapid pace and were soon completed and decorated throughout. I moved into my new office complete with my original desk and chair. The Company held their meetings in Jeff's office and sometimes I had to attend. Work from various areas was coming in very quickly, so Jeff took on more workmen, several carpenters and joiners and general labourers. We were still carrying out works for the Estate, work which had been approved before the takeover.

There were quite a few changes over the first few years with Albert Gerrard passing away, Bill Hooper and Billy Wellon both left. Fred Gerrard finally retired and Brian Overton left, therefore new staff were taken on but a lot of work was put out to contract.

Things didn't always run smooth, there were ups and downs, although I think I had more downs during G W Coventry's time.

What with looking out for people trying to take the firm to task, and taking advantage of His Lordship, I don't know how the firm lasted as long as it did – it never had a chance. Too many taking and not enough giving. I spent some lonely nights in the Estate Office when I was Company Secretary, worrying about various jobs and money, although his was not my problem I still worried about it. The Directors never seemed to worry about anything. I think it was just my teaching by George Kingdon, who was as straight as a gun barrel, which got me through it, just. My late wife Mary deserved a medal for putting up with me through those years. Rest in peace, Mary.

When the Croome Estate Trustees had altered the existing stores at High Green, Lord Coventry's new company Croome Leisure took over the Hospital Site buildings to rear pheasant chicks amongst other things. His two partners in this were John Stone and David Drinkwater. The Hospital site buildings' partitions were knocked down and the walls power washed. Frames were made, with mesh fitted, and these frames were fitted to the existing door frames to various rooms. The young pheasant chicks were bought and put in the rooms. The Airmans' ward was used as a deep litter room and was alive with chicks, then large incubators were installed in order to rear their own pheasants. Alas, this project never went the way it should have, some say the young pheasant chicks were being stolen, but by all accounts it was the gamekeeper taking them. David Drinkwater was then Managing Director of Croome Leisure. In the end his Lordship called an halt to this little venture.

The building opposite the Ambulance Station, the former Decontamination Rooms, had been turned into a Shooting Lodge. A fireplace was built with a chimney stack and a bar was installed. Toilets were also installed and the drains connected to the old RAF system which had not worked for years, consequently they were always getting blocked. By all accounts there were some wild parties after the days shoot. There was already an electric supply coming into these buildings, all they had to do was install lighting and points and reconnect to the electrical supply. Once again this came to a halt once the leisure and shoot stopped.

Once Croome Leisure had finished, these buildings remained empty. I was informed that they were going to be demolished and the land returned to agriculture. This did not happen. When they had vacated the Hospital site the Airmen's Ward was then used to store large timbers and stone floor slabs salvaged from an old building on the Estate. It could have been off the Barn at Chevington Farm.

It was then decided by Lord Coventry, John Stone and David Drinkwater, the Directors of Croome Leisure, that Pirton Pool should be turned into a trout fishing business. Jeff Jenks was instructed to drain the existing water over twenty eight acres, from the pool. One afternoon a low loader arrived at the yard with a large excavator on board. When I asked what was going on, Jeff said they were going to drain the pool, not by the correct way which would have been to pull the plug, but to make a large hole in the embankment and let the water go out. No thought was given to the large stock of fish in the pool. He told me that it would take too long to drain the pool using the plug, so the hole was put in the embankment and out roared the water. Some fish and eels were saved but many were killed and the herons had a feast. Fish were even stranded up in the hedges. It was a terrible sight. Along Pirton Lane there was two and a half foot of water. I was getting phone calls at home at night saying a water main had burst, but no, it was the water from Pirton Pool. I think the directors thought it was a big joke, if so it was a joke which could have backfired and put them all in jail. Not long after Pirton Pool was emptied, Jeff Jenks got the sack from G W Coventry Ltd and I was put in charge of the building company, therefore dealing with the Pirton Pool project.

The first job to do was to start ordering plant, diggers, excavators, Volvo earth moving machines, plus large tractors and trailers to move the excavated materials in the pool area. I dealt with a firm called Zenith Plant Hire from Station Road, Pershore. Mrs Marie Jones was the Manager and she got nearly all the machines from either Zenith or else she cross hired. David Drinkwater was going to deal with the dead trees around the pool area. The machines not only worked during the week but also at weekends and of course this took a lot of my time. We had a few ups and downs with the drivers on site with fights breaking out when they visited the Fruiterers Arms on Stonehall Common. In one instance a driver's leg was broken and an ambulance was sent for. Then we had quite a few batteries stolen from the machines and a main phone line was damaged. During this time David Drinkwater was nowhere to be seen. G W Coventry's workforce completed their work installing extra overflow drainage and some islands in the pool which were planted ready for the wildlife to take over. The original wooden plug was found and set up near the end of the pool by the overflow culvert. I got a brass plate made and inscribed and then fitted and the pool once again filled. The final job involved getting new steel gates fitted and these are still there, with pedestrian gates fitted alongside. It took a lot of my hard work and time, and I can't say it was wasted but it would have been nice to have seen the project take off. Eventually the firm folded. Before the time Jeff had been sacked he had started the Pirton Pool project and now it was up to me to get things going again. A big opening was staged and quite a few well known people came including Chris Tarrant. My job was complete and the water filled up the pool and it all looked very good. Sadly, Croome Leisure did not last very long and David

Drinkwater was dismissed, another sad story and another of Lord Coventry's companies coming to grief.

As I have said, Lord Coventry took over another building site for eight new houses in Corse Lawn, near Tewkesbury. The roads were already in but the builders had gone bust. They were taken over and the new company was called Arnlaw Developments and again Jeff Jenks was made Managing Director. Jeff Jenks was put in charge of this company to build eight houses on the new site. He set up a site office at Corse Lawn. I was made a director of G W Coventry Ltd and put in charge of the building works from High Green. Jeff Jenks had a Site Office on site at Corse Lawn. Ron Woodyatt then went to Corse Lawn as Foreman. The next man to appear was Len Pinnock, he too was a director of Arnlaw and also Managing Director of a timber framed building firm at Withington near Hereford. This company was called Pinacle, another company Lord Coventry bought out when they had gone to the wall. Mr Pinnock also became a Director of the insurance firm Lord Coventry had taken over in Birmingham.

G W Coventry had a full time architect working for them by now and his name was Roger Coneybeare. He was very good at his job but you couldn't very often get him away from the coffee cup. He produced some very good drawings for Pirton New Farm House, and Earls Croome Court's new pool house building amongst others.

Returning to the tale about G W Coventry Ltd, although my job was now book keeping, little whispers kept coming back to me that a lot of works were being undertaken and it was felt that the management did not know much about the building trade. Several sites were being left in an untidy state, and complaints from tenants had started coming in.

Lord Coventry decided that a new drive should be installed from the front of Earls Croome Court up to the main A38 road. The directors in charge were Kerry Hamer and Jeff Jenks. There was already a drive there but it was just grass and led to a pair of wooden gates at the A38. My job was to order the plant machinery. The job started, a new drive was dug out and new edging boards were made in the joinery shop complete with fixing pegs. There was a new turning circle to be installed at the front of the house. For the base of the new drive, they were going to use crushed tarmac waste from Defford Airfield which had now closed. I told Jeff Jenks I felt this was the wrong material to use as, back in the Estate's time, we had tried it and it was not a success because it would not compact down enough. Jeff did use it though, and Kerry Hamer got hold of a gipsy firm to put the tarmac down, then it was finished off with three-eighths pea gravel. After two months we had to make some notice boards to slow vehicles down to five miles per hour. The drive was like a roller coaster, up and down. Lord Coventry was not very happy about this. All of the drive had to be dug up and the materials dumped at the yard. The drive was started again. I ordered quarry waste to go into the base of the drive, which was then compacted with a heavy roller. I got a contractor from Coleford to come and give us a price for laying the tarmac and the price was accepted. Davis from Coleford in Gloucestershire were the contractors and they brought their Barber Green Tarmac Machine and the drive was completed and a good job carried out. Pea gravel was spread thinly over the new tarmac. Lord Coventry was pleased. I don't know how much it cost but if it had been done properly in the first place, it would not have cost half as much. I think Jeff Jenks left the company during this time, so it was left to me to complete the drive.

Later there was a board meeting at High Green, which I did not have to attend because it was to do with Arnlaw Developments at Corse Lawn. In attendance were Lord Coventry, Jeff Jenks, Mr & Mrs Kerry Hamer, Mr Pinnock with Christine Morgan taking notes.

I was sat in my office, I had now moved into Jeff Jenks office as he was stationed at Corse Lawn and the architect had moved into my office. Sitting at my desk, sorting out various papers, I heard Jeff's car start up and roar off the Estate yard, followed not long after by the Hamers. I didn't think things had gone too well.

Later Mr Pinnock came to my office and started talking to me about a property he had purchased at Red Marley, Gloucestershire, a big old house called Compton House. Not long after he left, this was on a Friday afternoon, before I had locked up the office, the phone started ringing and it was Jeff Jenks who accused me of telling Lord Coventry about various things. I told him I did not know what he was talking about, he was very angry at the time and slammed the phone down. He was in a very threatening mood. Just after 6.30 that same evenin,g Mr Pinnock came over to my house, No. 8 High Green, and said he had left some papers in my office, so we went to collect them. I told him that I had had the phone call from Jeff and Mr Pinnock said as he was staying with Lord Coventry that night he would mention it to him. Off he went, I returned home and that was that.

On the next day, Saturday, (when the office closed, the firm's phone was always switched to my house) the phone started ringing and I thought it might be more business for the Company but no, it was Lord Coventry, who said that he had sacked Jeff Jenks on that Friday night and I was told that I was to take over the running of G W Coventry Ltd and complete the new housing development at Corse Lawn. This was quite a shock to my system. My wife Mary came downstairs and asked me what was going on and she could not believe what had happened. Mary and I were great friends with Jeff and his wife Avril and had been to many functions with them. I just could not think straight at the time. By lunchtime it had sunk in that I had got a very big job on my hands, but I had had quite a few challenges since 1976. I then went over to my office and started sorting out various bits of paperwork ready for Monday morning. I had decided that I would have to have all the workforce on the yard at 8am and inform them what had happened.

Monday morning came very quickly and I spoke to the workforce in the joiners' workshop. I also told them the Estate yard gates would now be locked during the weekend and I think most of them were pleased. Jeff and his mates were always doing things at the yard at weekends and taking materials from the stores without telling me. I then had to speak to Roger Coneybeare, our architect about the Corse Lawn project. Some of the eight houses being built were being lived in including No. 8 which Jeff Jenks was supposed to have bought. I was told that I was to let Roger deal with the site until Jeff moved out. His Lordship thought there might be trouble if I called at the site. Jeff had got three company cars and they all had to be returned to Croome Estate yard and as I couldn't go, Roger and two other drivers were sent to collect them. They were returned in time, but the interiors had been left in a filthy condition. It looked as if Jeff had let his three dogs loose in every one. They were all sent to be valeted and then were returned to Birmingham, to Lord Coventry's other company. Jeff did take G W Coventry Ltd to court for unfair dismissal, a hearing which I had to attend, but it was thrown out.

Major works were undertaken at Lord Coventry's home Earls Croome Court at this time, all under my supervision. When completed, there was a party laid on at the Pool House attended by Court staff and the building firm's staff, and Lord Coventry with Miss Birch, his fiancee, soon to be the third Countess of Coventry. I had to make a speech to express thanks to the Earl of Coventry and Miss Birch for laying on a lovely spread.

Mr Pinnock had bought this large house in Red Marley,

Gloucestershire and during alterations he tried to use a lot of materials from the Arnlaw Developments site at Corse Lawn. This site was nearly completed and quite a few materials had been left on there. I had instructed the foreman there, Ron Woodyatt, to keep a note of everything being taken by Mr Pinnock, hence he received an invoice for all goods.

During the building of the new farm house at Pirton Court, Mr Pinnock got involved in scaffolding hire. During the course of the works he reported to me that some of his scaffold had been stolen and I was to inform the police and our insurance company, but when I went to the site one Sunday morning, Mr Peter Baxter informed me that Mr Pinnock had been there one night and collected a load of scaffold. Good job for him I had not informed the police, although I did inform Lord Coventry of both matters. Not long after this Mr Pinnock got the sack.

The next thing that happened was Lord Coventry asked Mary and me to dinner at Earls Croome Court. During the evening his Lordship took me into his study and informed me that he had asked the Fraud Squad to investigate Jenks and over the next week or two I would be getting a call from the police to arrange their visit. This was a very worrying time for me. Although I had done nothing wrong, a lot of questions were going to be asked of me and lots of paperwork had got to be produced. The day came and two Fraud Squad Officers came to the office. They told me what they required, which I duly produced. Christine Morgan was still the secretary of the Company and we had to give the police all the information we had. This was a terrible time for me. I had to hand over my duties of sorting the workmen's jobs to Roger Coneybeare because I was not allowed to leave the office. In between all this I had to attend meetings with Lord Coventry's solicitors. The meetings were held in the evenings at Earls Croome Court. After two weeks the Fraud

Squad officers had completed their investigation and I was very pleased that everything was ok.

Two weeks later Lord Coventry informed me that the police had got enough evidence to arrest Jenks and take the case to Crown Court, so there were meetings with solicitors and barristers that I had to attend and I had to sign various forms after thoroughly reading them. Once again a very worrying time for me. The court case was at Hereford and I was first in the witness box. It was very strange seeing Jeff come up from the cells between two police officers. I gave my evidence and by 3pm I was on my way back to Croome. I think there were nine or ten people giving evidence against Jeff, including His Lordship.

We were all shocked to learn that at the end of the week at court, Jeff was found not guilty on several charges and he was released. In one way I was pleased he had not had to go to jail, because we had been very good friends. A sad end though, to a good friendship.

In time Jeff Jenks moved from Corse Lawn and I was allowed to visit the site. Some people had already purchased their houses and moved in. We started getting problems with the drainage system, which had been put in incorrectly, and this cost His Lordship a lot of money to have corrected. Then we had problems with the gas flue liners as one family were nearly gassed due to the liners not being sealed. A really bodged job all round, once again costing Lord Coventry money to correct. More sleepless nights for me because I had to find other contractors who could put things right. Jeff had been on site all the time so this sort of thing should not have happened.

Once Corse Lawn was finished and the roads to the Estate were all completed and handed over to Highways, we set about moving all the surplus building materials, plant and other items back to the Estate yard.

Things were moving very fast and I had an awful job to keep up with it all. I wished I could go back to the easy way of dealing with the Estate, but that was not going to happen. Eventually the Corse Lawn houses were completed and sold off, so was the Hereford company, and G W Coventry stopped trading in 1986.

When the Hare Krishnas' bought Croome Court, you can imagine the talk that went round the local villages. G W Coventry got involved with them through Mr Albert Edwards, the caretaker, who had been at Croome Court during the Roman Catholics time. When he phoned me and asked if I was interested in pricing some works for the Hare Krishnas, I jumped at the chance to get some local work. Roger Conybeare who was the company architect came with me and we met up with Jnanagamya for the first of many visits to the Court. There were a lot of works undertaken roofing, lead flashing, showers in the bedroom, top of the house and many more jobs. The Hare Krishnas always paid their accounts on time. In the end G W Coventry carried out day to day maintenance at the Court. Jnanagamya sat and talked with myself regarding using G W Coventry as main contractors, so work was coming in regularly. Jnanagamya and I became very good friends and I was sorry when they moved to Watford.

There was never a dull time with the Hare Krishnas at Croome. In 2010, twenty five years after the Hare Krishnas left Croome Court, I am again in touch with Jnanagamya now by email and I have also given his email address to Eileen Clements who is a friend of Croome and hopefully she will learn a lot from him.

In January 1973 Col. Osbert passed away, a very sad loss to the Estate. During my time as storekeeper Mr Kingdon had shown me various timber planking which Col. Osbert had chosen off the Estate some years before, ready for his funeral. All the timber was banded at the ends by the Estate carpenters. When the sawmills had been moved from the opposite side of the road and re-erected behind the joiners' shop, it was one of my jobs to make sure that these timbers were transferred to new racking and not used for any other work. When Col. Osbert Smith passed away it was arranged that the undertaker from Upton-upon-Severn come to see me and he took the planks away so that the coffin could be made.

The funeral was a major event. Four of the Estate workers were bearers, some from the forestry department and some from the building department. The funeral was held at Earls Croome Church, and as the Colonel was an ex military man his coffin was draped with the Union flag. The Colonel was then cremated and his ashes laid to rest in Earls Croome churchyard. His grave and his parents are next to Lady Maria's grave at Earls Croome. Also under Col. Osberts slab are the remains of Col. Anthony Smith, his cousin. When this happened I thought that it was the end of the Estate, he was a wonderful man and his heart was at Croome, he was Croome.

Lord Coventry, the eleventh Earl, came to supper at No. 8 High Green many times with Mary and I during the 1980s. After our meal we would often sit in the lounge having a drink. One night the electric went off Mary got the candles lit and as we then had an open fire, we sat there until midnight with still no electric. Eventually Kevin and Caroline came home and sat with us. We all laughed and joked together. He really enjoyed his night with us. When he left he said we were his family. I will always remember his words. His Lordship was not yet married to his third wife at this time. He was a wonderful man. His Lordship also attended my father's funeral at Worcester which was a lovely gesture.

Eventually his Lordship married again and his wife Valerie was also a regular visitor to No. 8 High Green, after his Lordship introduced her to Mary and I. We all got on very well. It certainly got people talking when she used to park her Rolls Royce outside our cottage We have also had some good nights out with the pair of them and always finished up at his home at Earls Croome Court.

During Mary's illness his Lordship could not have been kinder. He or Valerie would pick Mary up and take her to Cheltenham for treatment. He also paid for her to have a private room at Southbank and at Droitwich so Mary could have surgery. Yes, I have lots to thank him for and I think that is why I have given so much back to Croome, his Estate at that time.

London Lodge was a target for lead thieves in the 1980s. The lead ridge was taken and we did not re-use lead but used new blue wall cappings. This property at the time was owned by Mr Buxton of Period and Country Homes

The Panorama was another target for the thieves when the main entrance door was always being broken in to. A much stronger door was made and covered with sheet materials. Two padbolts were fitted inside the building secured by two padlocks. Once secure, a ladder was erected from outside so the one who was securing the building had to exit the building by ladder. This stopped a lot of break ins.

Lord Coventry sold Flower Garden Cottage to John Stone who not only farmed High Green Farm, but also Kinnersley Farm. G W Coventry carried out the alterations to the cottage in the early 1980s, new bathroom, kitchen and other works. In Croome Estate Builders' time a new gravel entrance drive was put in complete with edging kerbs and a turning area to the front of the house and a new conservatory was built. When John Stone passed away, his wife decided not to stay and the cottage was once again sold. Another Estate property lost.

When the Hare Krishnas sold Croome Court, a man by the name of Sobey took over. He planned to run the Court as a learning and teaching school for a government backed project to enable unemplyed youngsters to learn various trades. It was called Manpower Services. G W Coventry was asked to carry out various works at the Court through Mr Edwards who was still caretaker and now employed by Sobey. Firstly we altered various rooms in the quadrangle and turn them into classrooms. Electrical work was carried out, new power points installed ready for the computers. The building which had been used as the Temple by the Hare Krishnas was turned into a clubhouse complete with a bar etc. A new security building was built. Down in the basement new floors were put in to make a dining room for the boys, new hot plates were fitted and all the meals were prepared in the basement. The lads came from all over the country and I do not think they had been away from home before or seen the countryside. My late son worked for Mr Sobey on the building staff, and he told me about damage they caused not only in the Court, but in the Rotunda which they nearly set on fire.

Eventually, due to non-payment of invoices, G W Coventry withdrew their labour (we never did get paid). All the staff were eventually made redundant, Mr Sobey went into Receivership, but then opened the Court as a hotel. The old library was fitted out with all the necessary kitchen equipment, and a new bar was manufactured and fitted in the Yellow Drawing Room. But the workmen who made this bar never got paid. The hotel did not last many weeks before ceasing trading. Mr & Mrs Sobey were rehoused in a bungalow at Birtsmorton near Malvern by the local district council. There was a picket line held outside the London Arch by myself and other firms who had never been paid for their servcies, but to no avail.

Croome Estate Builders 1986 until 1996

I was called to a meeting in the Estate Office boardroom. Col. Anthony Dudley Smith (Trustee), Mr Peter Pierpoint (Trustee), Mr Louis Shaffer (Trustees' Accountant) and Mr John Henderson (the Trustees' Agent), were all present. I was informed that Lord Coventry's Building Company, G W Coventry Ltd was going to be wound up and he, Lord Coventry, had talked to the Croome Estate Trustees regarding his decison. I was asked by Mr Shaffer if I would be prepared and could I, run a building firm owned by the Trustees. My response was "Yes". I was told that it was a big task to take on. The Trustees did not want to lose the building firm because it gave good service, not only for the upkeep of Estate properties but also to private clients. Col. Anthony and Peter Pierpoint were really excited about their new venture, both came to my office after the meeting and talked to me privately.

I had to resign as a director of G W Coventry Ltd and was made Manager of the new firm which was to be called Croome Estate Builders. Firstly I was told to write out my notice as director of G W Coventry Ltd. The next thing I had to do was to sell my company car and all the old vehicles which belonged to G W Coventry Ltd.

During the changeover, I had to inform our architect Roger Coneybeare that he would not be required by the new firm and therefore would be made redundant, but he was given his car. He was very good at his job, although, as I have said before, you could not move him from the office and his coffee cup. He had designed the alterations to Earls Croome Court, designed the new Pool House at Earls Croome Court and the new farmhouse for Pirton Court and many other jobs, but he had only one pace of working – slow. He did not take the decision to release him from his position very kindly and called at my home at High Green and threatened me with all sorts of things, but in the end, all went well. I do not remember who my secretary was at this time but she was to keep her job and so would all the workmen who had been employed by G W Coventry Ltd.

After selling off all the company vehicles, Croome Estate Builders took on new Mazda vehicles from Baynhall Garage. My car was a Mazda 323 and there were also a 1 ton pick-up and a 1 ton van – all Mazdas. The pick-up and van were cream in colour. On one Saturday morning I had arranged with a firm called City Signs to come and signwrite the two vehicles in Croome brown. I then arranged a write up in the local paper regarding the name change of the company. Most of our suppliers and contractors supported us.

The newspaper spread helped in our getting quite a few enquiries. The first I had was from the agent at Spetchley Estate a Mr Simon Wilton, and then Velcourt Properties, Madresfield Estate and Worcestershire County Council Property Department. We also received work from Sun Alliance, Lord Coventry and from John Henderson (Agent for the Croome Estate Trustees). I also carried out surveys for the Estate for various property service repairs. Croome Estate Builders got paid for my time doing the surveys and for my secretary typing up the works to be carried out. We then had to tender for these works as no favours were given – if our price was too high, we lost the contract.

We won a contract from the then owners of part of the Estate, Sun Alliance, to carry out major works to the south end of Croome river. This was not only to clear mud and weed near the Island but also to attend to some trees which had fallen into the river. Firstly we dug a channel just below the causeway to bypass the sluice and to enter the ditch beyond. Plant was hired from Zenith, including excavators and dumper trucks. An area in the nearby woodland was earmarked to receive the rubbish from the river, several rotten trees were removed and stacked ready for cutting up for firewood. The area around Island Pool was like a jungle and you could not see the excavator at work until he had cleared a path. The sluice was opened and what water went out was quickly sent down the open ditch. The fish were caught in nets and returned to the river beyond the causeway. The work was carried out when water in the river was at its lowest. Once the water had drained out, the dumper trucks were allowed to work from the island river bed. The mud and reeds were all conveyed to the site made ready in the wood nearby and dead trees were removed from the island. Repairs were carried out to the sluice ironwork at this time. There was quite a difference once the water had refilled the river and island area. The photos I took during these works are now

Malcolm Walford, 1987

with the Croome Estate office.

The carpenters workshop had no up-to-date machinery. There was a multi midsaw machine, with no guards on it and so it was very dangerous. I remember years ago Albert Gerrard, our top joiner on the Estate, having an accident and losing several fingers. The morning the accident had happened there had been a severe frost and you could see it glistening on the inside tiles as at that time the shop had no ceiling it was very cold, with no heating apart from a large wood fire.

In the 1940s, the old woodworking machine used to be in the old sawmill which was on the other side of the road opposite the Estate Office. The ground is now a village green. The old sawmill was taken down in 1968 and re-erected by the now joiners' shop. There was a lane which used to run to the sawmills, behind the old red telephone kiosk and alongside No. 8 High Green's hedge.

Eventually I took on a new joiner-cum-machinist, a lad called Colin Pettifer and got the okay from the Trustees to buy new machines. Colin and I went to Tewkesbury Saw Co. and looked at various machines and eventually agreed on three second hand machines – a new woodworking machine, cross cut and a new machine for cutting and mitreing timber. We could now make any joinery which was required; purpose made windows, doors, architraves and skirting boards. We also purchased a new dust extractor unit. The old machine was sold and the new machines installed.

We then had another enquiry. It was from Hindlip Agricultural College and the Principal's name was Mr Rob Brighton and eventually we were very lucky and got lots of work from there.

With the increase in works, I had to talk with Col. Anthony regarding the possibility of taking on an Assistant Manager. At a Trustee's Meeting it was agreed to advertise the position. We had quite a few applicants who were interviewed by myself and John Henderson, and agreed that the man who suited the position best was Mr Sid Hudson. Sid had worked for Wychavon District Council and was up to date with repairs and improvements to cottages and farms and had supervised quite sizeable jobs. I was looking forward to having some help and consequently a reduction in my workload – how wrong I was.

Works were now going at a pace, I had to increase the staff and office. Mrs Christine Hewitt was my secretary at this time so we took on another lady Mrs Kerry Paul, to answer the phone and do other bookwork including ordering materials etc. We also took on carpenters, bricklayers, painters and general labourers. With the increase in staff we had to increase vehicles. A small van was purchased for Sid Hudson's use, another one ton Mazda van and a pick-up (tipper). All had to be signwritten.

We next purchased mobile phones, the very old type which had to be charged up every night, and a new internal phone system was installed in all offices. The main phone would be in Mrs Paul's office and the rest of the offices had extensions. I, in my office, also had a phone belonging to Croome Estate on which John Henderson could speak to me when necessary.

One job we undertook was for the Croome Estate Trustees at St Kenelms Church, Upton Snodsbury. We had already secured the contract for re-roofing the Chancel and during the stripping of the roof tiles, things started going wrong. Sid Collins came back to the office at 5pm and suggested that I visit the site as soon as possible. I informed Pip Webster, the Assistant Agent, (John Henderson was at a Meeting in London at the time) that I had a problem at the Church and I would be going there straight away. Sid and I arrived at the Church at about 6pm and looked at the problem which was at the stone gable end of the Church near the road. Because we had stripped the roof tiles off the Chancel, it had caused the gable end of the wall to move out about two inches. I immediately took the decision to call out Emergency Building Services from Welland, a firm I had used before run by a Brian Virgo. We, Croome Estate Builders, had not got the manpower to tackle this work. Mr Virgo arrived at the site at 8pm, he arranged for a scaffolding firm who arrived about 9.30 and they started putting up shoring to the gable wall. I also had to inform the police regarding closing off the road in case of any accident. I eventually returned home at 11pm. After several months and a lot of worry, the works were completed by the contractors. The whole gable end had to be taken down and rebuilt, including the stained glass window. The re-roofing of the chancel was completed by Croome Estate Builders. During the works, we had made sure that church services could still be carried out as we had boarded up the opening left by the huge window. After all the works were completed and the site cleaned up, I was informed that I would have to give a speech to the congregation. This I did one Sunday evening – quite a nerve racking experience for me. This job had cost thousands of pounds, but a good job had been carried out to the approval of all the Trustees.

After Mr Sobey left Croome Court it was sold to Mr Christopher Buxton of Period and Country Homes. Croome Estate Builders carried out various works to both the Court and the surrounding buildings, including the stable block, Priest House, and what had, in the Coventry's time, been the old indoor riding school, also London Lodge and the Marble Arch. We also located the original main gates to the entrance. Our main job was to keep the buildings watertight, replacing lead flashings, and making roof repairs to the London Lodge when the lead was stolen from the ridges. My late son Kevin was employed by Mr Buxton and carried out various works, gardening, chainsawing, inspecting and clearing the filter beds (on

Malcolm Walford, 1990

the south side of the park), and most of all dealing with the main pumps which not only took away sewage but also some stormwater. When Kevin moved into a flat at Croome, he had a bell which warned him during a storm that the pumps would need to be started. These pumps were on their last legs and were going to be replaced, but unfortunately Mr Buxton sold up before this happened.

We carried out a few large contracts, but then came the slump in the building trade and unfortunately we had to start laying off some staff.

Because of the staff reductions, I let out the joinery workshop to a lad who worked for us, Donald Mackenzie. The next place I rented out was Sid Hudson's office plus some storage area on the yard to a local firm called TCG Painting Contractors. Their owner was Ty Lancaster. The rent went to Croome Estate Trustees, not the building firm. Once I had sorted things out I promoted Sid Collins to General Foreman. Sid was a bricklayer by trade but had worked for himself and knew how to run and organise sites, so things were up and running again. With Sid running the sites it meant that I could get on with surveying and estimating, but I still visited the sites to check that all was going well and talk to people to find out if there were any complaints, although none were reported.

My late son worked at Croome Court for various owners on the maintenance team. He, like me, loved Croome. He would always be talking about Croome and what he had been doing during his day's work. Kevin was a good caretaker during the time Croome was not lived in and was well liked by Mr Buxton, who had every faith in him. Kevin and I spent many a weekend just walking around Croome. When he took on the job as gardener for the Croome Estate Trustees at Levant Lodge, he certainly put some effort into getting the garden up and running, but it was never appreciated by some people. He was very good at his job. I wish he was still here today. They say time heals, but I do not feel that way, the one thing is, he will never grow old.

During heavy rain and with the Severn overflowing its banks, the call went out regarding safeguarding the inside of St Denys Church, Severn Stoke. John Henderson, who was agent for the Croome

Receiving the 40 years' service medal, 1995

Estate and a church warden there, requested help. At the Estate Yard in High Green, we had two bays, one for gravel and sand, the other for building sand. In the evening, in heavy rain and in pitch darkness we were asked to fill a lot of sand bags. Kevin and I worked in awful conditions to fill these and get them to Severn Stoke Church.

Clive Gittins arrived on one of his tractors because by now the flood water was up to the A38 road. Kevin and I put the sandbags in the bucket of the tractor and Clive drove to the Church with Kevin and I both hanging on to the side of his tractor. Once we got to the Church, we carried the sandbags to the various parts of the Church stumbling in the darkness over graves. The sandbags were all laid but sadly the water entered the Church and did quite a lot of damage, although we did try our best.

We were rewarded for our efforts in due course. It is all right working in the daylight but in the pitch blackness and driving rain, it was not much fun, but this was our local Church which we wanted to save. Unfortunately flooding has happened at Severn Stoke for many a year.

Into the 1990s

When a gardener's job became available at Levant Lodge in 1990, I told my son Kevin and he applied for the position. I had a word with Col. Anthony Smith regarding Kevin and told him that I would be very proud if Kevin got the position as it would be in the Walford tradition of keeping in touch with the Coventry family. He did eventually get the position and in due course quite transformed the garden at Levant. He grew vegetables for the house, and also for Col. Anthony when he stayed at the Coach House for two or three nights a week, and which he would take back to Bradford on Avon where he lived. During my time as Manager of Croome Estate Builders and at a slack period, I asked Col. Anthony Smith if the workmen could go to the Croome Churchyard and tidy up. This he agreed to because he, like his late cousin, Col. Osbert, loved Croome. Around the perimeter of the churchyard there were several dead elm trees and lots of brambles. Col. Smith also said that Kevin could help out with a chain saw.

Reg Child drove the tractor and trailer and Sid Collins was in charge of the works. Firstly the elm trees were cut down and then cut into lengths ready to be loaded on the trailer. Lots of the timbers were cut into sizeable logs and the men were allowed to share them between themselves for their home fires. All the brush was burnt and there were several bonfires lit. The brambles were cleared from the iron railings, these too were burnt and the churchyard began to look tidy. There were some dead trees at the top west of the churchyard and these too were cut down and cleared. Sid Collins also repaired a couple of gravestones at this time, one belonging to an old Estate bricklayer, whom I had known when I started at Croome, Herbert Page. Since these works have been done, the cowslips and other wild flowers have returned to the churchyard.

In 1996 Kevin, moved into a small building adjoining the Priest House at Croome Court when he was working for Mr Buxton. His job was to look after Croome Court which was now unoccupied. Mr Edwards, the old caretaker, and his wife were still living at the Court. Kevin loved living there and knew all about the Court workings, from the main sewerage works to the rainwater drainage. During Mr Buxton's time he allowed the Police to use the Court for dog training. Kevin would hide in various parts of the Court, the police would then release the dogs to track him down. They generally found him, but he never got bitten.

Kevin took many photos of the Court, which I have in an album. These will be left to the Croome Estate Trustees when I pass on.

In 1996 the Trustees decided to wind up the building firm Croome Estate Builders. This was not many days after the passing of Col. Anthony Smith, the senior Trustee. The staff had to be made redundant, I had to sell all the vehicles, woodworking machines and all of the builders' plant. On completion of this I gave up my office and moved part of my office equipment to Levant Lodge, the then home of Lady Maria Coventry. My equipment was housed in the staff quarters.

The garden side of the job was the lawn mowing, cutting firewood for the house, repairs to the stockproof fencing, arranging contractors to cut main hedges and tree surgeons to fall any dead or diseased trees. Ivor Jones and Bill Holland carried out works at Levant Lodge before I moved there full time, and then when they left I took on a man from Kempsey, Eddie Thompson and Gordon Collins joined us later. We carried out a lot of external works and Lady Maria was really excited about what was going on. In the autumn, another job we had was to pick all the apples and store them for winter use in the house.

Croome Estate Trustees' Employees who worked for the Estate Building Department in the late 1950s to 60s and are still with us today are:

Billy Wellon	– Handyman *(also worked for the nuns at Croome Court)*
Ron Woodyatt	– General Labourer
Bob Northcott	– Carpenter
Brian Overton	– Estate M T Driver and Handyman
Donald Smith-Keitley	– Joiner/Carpenter
Norman Homer	– Painter and Decorator
Maurice Sherwood	– Apprentice Carpenter
Sidney Collins	– Bricklayer and later Foreman
Tom Campion	– General Foreman
Frank Tallit	– Handyman
Brian Hyatt	– Apprentice Bricklayer
Graham Saunders	– Apprentice Bricklayer
Malcolm Jones	– Painter
Clive Johnson	– Apprentice Carpenter

FORESTRY DEPARTMENT:

John Hodson	– Forestry Worker
Robert Fassnidge	– Forestry Worker
Ray Neathway	– Forestry Worker

In early 2007, due mainly to the hard work of Mr Peter Beresford, the Trustees as Croome Heritage Trust bought Croome Court back and it is now leased to the National Trust. Unfortunately later that year Lady Maria died, but she knew that the Court was once again back in the hands of the Trustees and the Coventry family and she was delighted.

I had to lay off the garden staff and Levant Lodge was put up for sale. What Col. Osbert Smith and Col. Anthony Smith would think about it, I really do not know. I continued working at the house after Lady Maria left us until 2009 and the new owners took over, but I had a funny feeling when in the garden, that she was there watching and not far away. You tend to ask yourself if she would like you cutting this shrub down. No doubt about it, Lady M is still at Levant Lodge. Her dogs are buried in the gardens, Pindy, and Rocky whom she loved so much. Everyone misses Lady M, she was a very special Lady. Lady M and Lord Coventry are both still greatly missed. They were two wonderful people.

Mr Beresford one of the current Trustees said he would like me to get involved with Croome Court now that they have bought it back into the Estate, and spend two mornings a week, meeting the National Trust visitors and telling them about my life on the Croome Estate and about the changes of ownership of Croome Court since the Coventry family left in 1949. I started this work on Wednesday 28 March 2012 and I am really enjoying it. I have also given a talk about my time at the Estate.

Where I now live, at the bungalow, I am surrounded by momentos of my time at Croome. Pictures in the sitting room are of Croome d'Abitot Church, a Lancaster Bomber flying over Croome, and a picture of Lady Maria and me on my fifty years presentation at the Three Counties Show at Malvern. Moving into the hall, there is a large picture of Croome Court and three pictures of myself and my presentation medals for forty, forty-five and fifty years service to Croome. There is also a model of the Croome Court Locomotive on the bookshelf.

In the dining room there is the original bell which was once upon a time attached to Pirton School. There also is a lovely painting by my nephew Alan Walford, of Pirton Church. Alas Alan passed away some time ago now, a very talented lad. There is also a photograph of me taken at Croome Estate on my retirement. Into the kitchen and another picture presented by the Croome Estate Trustees on my forty years of service to the Estate. In the small bedroom there is a photograph of the Croome Court Locomotive.

Up into the roof space and you find several boxes, the first one contains all my old diaries, external order books, materials used books and other items on Croome. In the second there are various photo albums i.e. the Builders Yard as it used to be and how it was after Croome Estate Builders stopped trading in 1996, that was a very sad day for all concerned.

In the garage I have my old Clerk of Works sign which used to be on the office door. I also have the original G W Coventry sign which used to be on the finger post opposite Croome Estate Yard. So you see, everywhere I turn I am reminded of Croome. But as I have said before, Croome is in my blood and I would do anything for Croome.

Drinking my glass of scotch at home in the conservatory, my mind wanders back to the time I started at Croome and the time George Kingdom put me in charge of the stores. I would like the National Trust to have the old diaries which I kept during my working life from 1953-1961 until I went into the office, together with my photo album of life on Croome.

One night, a couple of years ago now, Peter Beresford came to stay for the night, and before and after our meal we talked about various things and Croome was at the top of the agenda. We discussed my involvement with Croome and he was quite adamant that I had still a big part to play at there. I said I was honoured to be the last workman from 1953 to still be involved with Croome and I was very proud to have known so many loyal workmen who had served the

With Lady Maria Coventry at my 50 years presentation, 2004

Trustees and the Coventry family over the years, and I am honoured to be a spokesperson for all those who have passed on.

It is now nearly sixty years since I started on Croome Estate but lately I have been involved with sorting various items to be out on show at Croome Court for the National Trust. Peter Beresford wanted me to get involved with sorting out these items which had been stored in the loft over the agent's office for some years.

Firstly we got rid of all the empty cardboard boxes, flattened them and stacked them in my car. Then we started moving storage boxes which had various paperwork in them and stacked them with the rest of the so called 'chicken boxes' (which were used by the Estate to store various items). There were also quite a few tin boxes (probably old deed boxes), two signs regarding Croome Church and behind the largest we found some ironwork which I thought had gone to scrap in the 1950s. This ironwork used to be in the old Blacksmiths Shop and was held together by wooden rails. I had been told that the ironwork was made by Tommy Child the Estate blacksmith and were copies of that which used to be by the Punchbowl Gates. The original tops are still with these railings. I have informed Pip Webster, the agent, of my findings and hope they will be of some use to the National Trust at Croome Court. There were many old wooden signs made by the Estate carpenters, but not much more of interest only rubbish to go to the tip eventually.

We have already sorted out the original bronze fire bell which has the inscription 'To the Rt. Hon. Lord Coventry' engraved on it. There are several other items in the loft which may be of interest to the National Trust. I am really honoured that Mr Beresford has asked me to sort out these items. While I was helping out at Earls Croome Court, I managed to salvage some tin trunks which were used to store Coronation robes belonging to the Coventry family, which I am sorry to say were going to the tip. These are now with Gill Tovey at the Croome Estate Office. The Trustees also asked me if I would write my memoirs of working life on Croome Estate which I have now completed.

On a recent visit to the churchyard I visited Lady Joan Coventry's grave. At present the foxes or badgers are digging down the side of the grave and causing a problem, I have reported this back to the office for them to contact Jo Cross of the Churches Conservation Trust to see if she can help.

I am still dealing with and working for the Croome Estate and Estate properties, some not owned now by the Estate. Earls Croome Court which is now owned by Mr David Wickens was once the home of the eleventh Earl of Coventry and his wife. Lots of works are being carried out to improve the house after the theft of many oak doors and fireplaces. Many of the garden ornaments have been sold off. What a terrible thing to happen, still, things are coming together. New doors have been made and fitted, new ornaments are now in the grounds.

Over the last few years I have lost several old mates and it is very worrying. I have just heard that yet another of my youth club mates has passed away, and now there are only three of us left of the original Wadborough lads, myself, John Westmacott and young Terry Griffiths. We are all getting older. I have just had a read of my father's notes and he was writing the same thing – he was losing all his friends.

Recently another close friend of my family died, Fred Garrard who was the Estate forester and lived next door at No. 6 High Green when my family and I were living there. Fred and his wife Pearl, and their two children, Royston and Susan moved into the Estate foresters house next door in 1967. We all got on very well, and when Fred took up his duties as Head Forester he had an office next door to mine. I dealt with Fred when ordering timber off the Estate for the building department. Fred was buried with his wife at Severn Stoke Churchyard.

Looking back at my time at the Croome Estate, I have certainly lost a lot of old workmates. From when I started in 1953, there are only a couple of workmen left. I sometimes sit and think of my time at Croome and I get depressed looking back over the years, but as my late father used to say 'that's life'. It's not only losing my workmates, but also close friends I grew up with in Wadborough; Eddie Brixey, Ron Mills, Peter and John Griffiths, George Wilkes. Michael Westmacott, Nora Stamp, Phyllis Richings, Susan Smith – the list goes on for ever.

The other day whilst working for the Trust at Croome, I met up with David Kingdon, my old boss's son, and his wife. David was born in Ronkswood Hospital two days after my daughter Caroline.

I had not met David for such a long while and we exchanged addresses and promised to keep in touch. I took them on a tour of the Court and showed them the picture gallery in the basement. He has promised to send me a photo of his Dad. What a great morning we had, talking about when he was a young lad growing up with my son and daughter and also the son and daughter of Fred, the late forester, Sue and Royston Garrard. I have promised them if I reach my sixty years service in August 2013, they will both be invited to my party. God willing I reach this goal. My Uncle Bob who was forester on the Estate, completed fifty nine years and I am hoping I shall beat this record.

Recently I have taken parties of National Trust volunteers and Friends of Croome Court around Croome Estate Builders Yard at High Green. On one tour there was the former agent for the Estate, John Henderson and also John Chugg whose family farmed on the Estate and lived at Red Deer Farm. I know people are more interested in Croome Court and its progress, but Croome Yard and Offices were a hive of activity in my early years at Croome. This is where all the decisions were made regarding works at the Court and on the Estate. The offices are still there but there is only the Land Agent and her secretary working there now. The Estate is not as large as it was back in 1953, at that time you had an agent, sub agent, Estate clerk and two women secretaries. The forester was based in these offices, and the gaffer of the building department was in a small office in the Estate yard buildings. I also told of the large tanks where, on a wet day, we had to run lime putty, a very dusty and dirty job. I explained on these tours how the joiners' shop produced all the timber items required on the Estate, of the blacksmiths' and wheelwrights' shops and about how the office block changed in 1969 when new building were put up, which the National Trust are now using. I explained how the Hospital site buildings were used in 1961 as the main stores and how in 1969, when the yard buildings and the set up were improved, the stores were transferred back to the yard at High Green and how tidy I kept them. I also pointed out where the village Post Office had been and the off-licence pub, the Coventry Arms, all long gone. I talked about the blacksmiths and wheelwrights on the yard and what work they carried out, and of course all the old employees who were so loyal to this Estate. To see the Yard and inside of the buildings now makes me feel very low. I have never, in all my days at Croome, seen anything so untidy. I think it is a great shame how the site looks today, it will never be the same again.

I hope as you read my memoirs you will have some idea of how life was back in my younger days. My parents would have been proud of my long service for the Estate, and it is only perhaps by chance, that I came to work on the Estate after moving with my parents and brother to come and live in Wadborough in 1948. The Walford family as a whole go back a long way on the Estate and I am proud to have kept this long tradition alive. I shall still visit Croome Court and grounds and always be available to answer any questions I am asked by the visitors and the National Trust. I am always available if the Croome Estate Trustees require help with anything. I hope the people who read these memoirs will also get some pleasure from them and can share in what happened in the past on a large Estate such as Croome. I am glad to have put all this down on paper, otherwise tales such as mine will be lost for ever. I know that Croome Court is the top priority for the National Trust but what went on at the heart of the Estate also matters.

When I entered the Estate Office after my promotion in 1961, my whole life changed. Here we are in 2013, coming up to my sixty years service at Croome Estate. It is very hard to explain to people how I feel about Croome. I find it hard when people say to me 'Don't worry about things, let others deal with it'. I cannot be like that, my life has been Croome, I have always been there for Croome. Whether it has been floods, fire, blocked drains, leaking roofs, gales, damage to property, I have always responded to requests for help. This has always been and always will be the way I deal with things. I hope my parents and grandparents are proud of what I have achieved over my years at Croome.

Croome used to be one big family. You could not wish to work with any better or more dedicated men than the workmen I have worked with. They knew their jobs. Some were born into the Estate, served in the first and second World Wars and their jobs were always there for them on their return. Some also did National Service and then returned to work on the Estate. They lived their lives for the Coventry family and were in a class of their own.

I had a very good wife in Mary and two wonderful children, Kevin and Caroline. Alas Kevin was taken from me not long after his mom but I still think about them every day. I have two grandchildren, Crystal and Craig, who can be very trying at times, but I am still proud of them. I have had some good times with my family and some very hard times, living at Pirton and then High Green, but we got through the hard times. All families go through bad patches but love carries them on and you come up against the next challenge in life, and life certainly is challenging, and it has been hard at Croome at times especially during the early years.

The house at Croome Court is now open, the windows to the Temple Greenhouse have just been renewed and a very good job carried out by Carlton-Smith Joinery. I still visit Croome on a regular basis and hopefully will do so for some years to come. The Churches Conservation Trust officer, Joe Cross has approached me about getting involved with the tidying up of Croome Churchyard.

In 2012 Alice Padley of the National Trust wrote an article about me for the local paper, to celebrate my fifty nine years service on the

Estate and to the Coventry family. My thanks to Alice and also to Amy who took a photograph of me in the Court to go with the newspaper article.

It is hard to put into words how I feel about Croome. I am the only one who has written about these times, as I saw them happening, and I felt I must must write it down before it is all forgotten. I have been very close to the Coventry family and to both Col. Osbert and Col. Anthony Smith. Croome has been my whole family's life, I have no regrets. Croome took over my life completely in 1961 when I first entered the Clerk of Works office, and I think I have given loyal service to the Estate over the last sixty years. I hope I have given some insight into the hard work that the Estate staff had to contend with. My late father always said that there was something about Croome. I now know what he meant.

As I wander around Croome Park, my mind wanders back to the sixty years I have spent working for the Estate. I think of the times George Kingdon and I would walk around the grounds not only at weekends, but also on summer nights, the times when Mary my wife was working in the Court when it was the Boy's School. I look across at the Red Wing which hopefully will be restored now the National Trust have it. I think of my late son Kevin who worked at and loved Croome, the times I have been with him when he has been down in the pump house starting the pumps to clear the water and walking across to the filter beds.

In 2003 my wife Mary died and the following March my son joined her. They are both buried in the Churchyard at Severn Stoke along with my great grandson Tyler who was still born, so I have three to talk to when I visit which is usually once or twice a week. I have been told by the doctors not to visit so often, but I feel I have to. I feel I am letting them down if I do not visit them regularly. When my time comes my resting place will be with them at Severn

Stoke.

Should I reach the age of eighty in August 2013 I shall have worked for the Trustees and the Coventry family for sixty years. Let's hope I reach this goal.

Croome Court since the Coventry Family

1948-1949	The family left
1950-1979	Catholic School
1979-1984	Hare Krishna
1984-1987	Sobey, YTS/Hotel
1987-1993	Period & Country Homes, Mr Buxton
1993-1996	Mr Rudge & Partner
1997	Mr Butler *(sale never took place)*
1999-2007	Lawrence Bilton
2007-	Croome Heritage Trust/National Trust

I first was introduced to Viscount Deerhurst, the eleventh Earl of Coventry's son in 1963 when the then Countess of Coventry (Mimi) visited the Clerk of Works office with Col. Osbert Smith. Viscount Deerhurst had not long started school and he was in his grey school uniform. I have, since those early days, met Viscount Deerhurst several times at Earls Croome Court and at the Rose and Crown at Severn Stoke.

Over the years I have met and had to deal with all four of the eleventh Earl's wives:

1st wife:	Marie (Mimi) Farquhar Medart	1955-60
2nd wife:	Ann Cripps	1969-75
3rd wife:	Valerie Birch	1980-88
4th wife:	Rachel Wynn	1992

Viscount Deerhurst sadly died in 1997 at the age of forty.

The eleventh Earl of Coventry died in 2002 at the age of sixty eight

Lady Maria Coventry passed away in 2007

The first time I met the present Earl of Coventry (the thirteenth Earl) was at Levant Lodge, the home of Lady Maria when he used to come and stay at the annexe. We got on well from day one. I have not, as yet, had the pleasure of meeting his wife.

Well this completes my story of Croome, the place where I have worked for so many years and hopefully will keep getting involved with in one way or another.

Planting a tree with Peter Beresford, Trustee, Croome Estate,
24 November 2013